AFRICAN AMERICAN PRIDE

AFRICAN AMERICAN PRIDE

Celebrating Our Achievements, Contributions, and Enduring Legacy

Tyehimba Jess

CITADEL PRESS
Kensington Publishing Corp.
www.kensingtonbooks.com

CITADEL PRESS BOOKS are published by

Kensington Publishing Corp.
850 Third Avenue
New York, NY 10022

First printing: December 2003

10 9 8 7 6 5 4 3 2 1

Printed in the United States of America

Library of Congress Control Number: 2003113675

ISBN 0-8065-2498-7

Dedicated to the spirit of our African ancestors, and to
seekers of knowledge around the world.

Acknowledgments

Thanks to my father, Jesse Goodwin, for the extensive library at home. Thanks to my mother, Della McGraw, for staying up with me late at night and reading to me, making me believe I could actually read and write.

Thanks to my brother and sister for their encouragement along the way. Props to Quraysh Ali Lansana for the recommendation. Much thanks to the Cave Canem family, especially Sheree, and all my teachers along the way, particularly Edgar Epps and Sterling Plumpp.

Contents

Preface

Volumes have been written about African American history. This book should start you toward a basic understanding of several areas of African American life and history, and refer you to some basic sources for further research.

The subjects in this book were chosen for their relevance to black history and culture. The individuals I have profiled here were selected for their extraordinary accomplishments and stunning perseverance. Many other individuals could have been included in this book, but time and space restrictions have forced me to limit the book to the twenty-six individuals listed here.

I made an effort to feature as many women as men, to feature gay as well as straight individuals, and to provide some brief introduction to some of the major movements in our history in a beginning effort to describe the patchwork quilt of African American experiences. I hope this book will serve as a small piece of your ever-expanding blanket and armor of knowledge, a beginning toward a deeper understanding of a history and a people that have made fascinating and inspiring contributions to the history of humanity. Here, we read of a people that spent centuries in American slavery, another century in the apartheid of Jim Crow Laws, and still struggles against the mountainous forces of discrimination. Here, we read of a people whose struggle for human and civil rights has consistently been on the cutting edge of American social and political progress. I hope you enjoy this learning adventure.

Forwards Ever, Backwards Never . . .
Tyehimba Jess

HISTORICAL MOVEMENTS

Our African Heritage

Let us never forget where we come from, our connection with African people all across the world. All of our art, our dance, our genius, survival is owed to our African heritage. African American history is as old as humanity's history, as old as Egypt's pyramids and the ancient libraries of Timbuktu. Often, African Americans are made to feel as if their people have made no contributions to the world. Nothing could be further from the truth.

When we talk about our blues, we can trace the musical form back to Africa. When we talk about our unique twist of English, we can trace our gifted tongues back to the unique languages of Africa. When we revel in our dance, we can trace our steps back to the ethnic dance of the motherland. When we talk about the three major religions of the world, Christianity, Islam, and Judaism, we can trace them all back to the people of Africa. When we talk about the magnificence of the Egyptian pyramids, we are talking about an African Legacy. These are just a few of the many marvels that have originated from people of African descent.

While this book focuses on the history of Africans in America, it would be wise to check out how that history relates to Africans on their native continent and throughout the world.

Books to check out!

Introduction to Black Studies by Maulana Karenga
The Cultural Unity of Black Africa by Chiekh Anta Diop
The African Origin of Civilization: Myth or Reality by Chiekh Anta Diop
How Europe Underdeveloped Africa by Walter Rodney
Introduction to African Civilizations by John G. Jackson

The Middle Passage: Maafa

Only the strong survived. Under the turgid waters of the Atlantic Ocean, there is a trail of bones, the remains of African men, women, and children who died in the holds of slave ships on the way to the shores of the Caribbean and the United States. This trail of diseased, starved, broken, and beaten bodies was known as the Middle Passage, the trade route of slavery. Today, the Middle Passage and the centuries of African slavery that followed are described by the Kiswahili term for disaster, "Mafaa."

African people were either forcibly kidnapped by white slavers or traded to Europeans for cloth and other goods by contentious tribal leaders who were not familiar with the harshness of European slavery. Most slaves came from coastal West Africa, from the areas now known as Senegal, Gambia, Sierra Leone, Ghana, Benin, and Nigeria. Once aboard a slave ship, they were chained and crammed into dark holds with barely enough room to breathe. The defiant or sick were tossed overboard with the dead into a sea teeming with sharks. It is estimated that the continent of Africa lost from fifteen to twenty million souls during the carnage of the slave trade, and that up to one-third of these captives died on their way to the Americas and the Caribbean.

Those that survived the journey were subjected to brutality in a strange new world and treated as property, no more human than a pig, horse, or hammer. They survived through cunning, strength, and spirit. They were the muscle that built the economic power of the southland. Without it, the United States as we know it today would not exist.

Today, we remember the millions that did not survive the brutality of the Maafa, those who were starved and worked to death and dreamed of freedom. It is up to us to take advantage of that strength and spirit in order to manifest a full realization of our human potential today. We can best memorialize our ancestors in positive acts for our communities, through creating or joining effective organizations that enhance our career and education opportunities. It is up to us to make sure that our ancestors are not forgotten, and that we make the world a better and fairer place where all can prosper equitably.

Books to check out!

The Middle Passage: White Ships/Black Cargo by Tom Feelings
Black Imagination and the Middle Passage by Maria Diedrich
The Maafa and Beyond: Remembrance, Ancestral Connections and Nation Building for the African Global Community by Erriel D. Roberson

Steal Away: Black Abolitionists and the Underground Railroad

In the middle of the night throughout America's south, on any given night, groups of slaves followed the North Star through swamps, forests, heat, and cold in order to make it north to the free states on the other side of the Ohio River. The series of connections, hiding places, and safe houses they used along the way was known as the Underground Railroad.

The Underground Railroad was a singular act of courage by a loose conglomeration of determined outlaws, white and black—but the first step toward freedom was always taken by a black foot. Heroes such as **Frederick Douglass** and **Harriet Tubman** are some of the better-known "conductors" who labored to bring black folks out of bondage. Douglass smuggled himself out of the south and became an outspoken abolitionist and "general" of the Railroad. Harriet Tubman was a fugitive slave who first "stole herself" from her master's bondage in 1849, but then returned to free her sister, brother, parents, and at least 300 other slaves at the risk of death upon capture. In the Civil War, she served as a scout and nurse for the Union Army.

Other black abolitionists include **William Still,** executive director of the **Philadelphia Anti-Slavery Society.** Still sheltered and fed hundreds of slaves on their way to points north, away from slave hunters who stalked their prey on both sides of the Mason-Dixon Line. Still also wrote down their stories in an effort to help broken families reunite after slavery. He later published his 800-page tome, *The Underground Railroad,* in 1872.

Runaways were aided along the way by an ingenious code of spirituals, sung to warn or welcome them along the way, and quilts that were sewn in patterns that acted as signposts on the way. Without this crucial help from sympathetic blacks along the way, the Railroad would not have been as effective. Others developed more inventive ways to get off the plantation, like **Henry Box Brown,** who had a white sympathizer mail him to Philadelphia in a wooden box! He later published his story in *Narrative of the Life of Henry Box Brown.*

William Whipper and **Stephen Smith** were two of the wealthiest free blacks in the country in the 1830s. Founders of successful businesses in Columbia, Pennsylvania, they used much of their wealth to assist the Underground Railroad. Whipper ran a station on the Railroad from 1847 to 1859, and always encouraged his passengers to continue on to Canada.

Many runaways would not feel safe in the United States, and would not rest until arriving in Canada. One of the main destinations for many fugitives was Detroit, a place where they could cross a mile-wide river and arrive on Windsor's free soil. Today, when we stand on the edge of the Detroit River and see Canada on the other side, we can only imagine the thrill that must have been felt by those who had spent years in bondage and weeks or months evading slave catchers on their way to freedom.

Books to check out!

Slavery and the Underground Railroad: Bound for Freedom by Carin T. Ford
Let My People Go: The Story of the Underground Railroad and the Growth of the Abolitionist Movement by H. Buckmaster
The Black Abolitionist Papers, Vol. III: The United States, 1830–1846 edited by C Peter Ripley
The Black Abolitionist Papers, Vol. IV: The United States, 1847–1858 edited by C Peter Ripley

Maroonage: Runaway Slave Societies

While there were many that followed the North Star to Canada and the northern states in order to steal themselves away from slavery, there were also those that chose to set up outlaw communities deep in the forests and swamps of the south, right under the master's nose but out of his reach. These hidden outposts of freedom were known as maroon societies. In the **Dismal Swamp,** between Virginia and North Carolina, over 2,000 escaped slaves and their descendants formed a free community. These outlaws, whose only crime was to possess their own skin, carried on illegal trade with white residents on the swamp's fringes until the early 1700s. Another fugitive camp was located in the **Cypress Swamp** of Louisiana for at least three years until their leader, **Squire,** was captured and killed in 1836.

Because they were secret societies, we may never know exactly how many maroon communities existed in the south, but we do know that they were born under perilous conditions and were subject to frequent attack from slaveholders. Newspapers of the time hold accounts of maroons that were captured, but not of those that remained free. Many times maroon communities prospered for two to three years before being destroyed, captured, or disbanded and fading into the wilderness.

Probably the most famous example of marronage in the U.S. is the case of the **Seminole** nation of Florida, which accepted runaway slaves as partners in the fight against American invaders to their territory. Slaves had escaped to Florida since the late 1600s in order to gain freedom under Spanish law. After Spain seceded Florida territories to Britain in 1763, blacks continued to live among the Seminoles. Dade County, Florida, is named for the American Major Francis L. Dade, who was defeated in battle in the murky swamps of Florida with Seminoles in 1835. Famous black and Indian generals **John Horse** and **Wild Cat** led Seminoles into battle in desperate bids for freedom launched. The struggle of maroon communities is one we can be proud of for its ingenuity, strength, and refusal to despair under the harshest of circumstances. We must ask ourselves how we will match this drive for freedom today.

Books to check out!

Exiles of Florida—or, the Crimes Committed by Our Government Against the Maroons Who Fled from South Carolina and Other Slave States Seeking Protection under Spanish Laws by Joshua Giddings

Maroon Societies: Rebel Slave Communities in the Americas edited by Richard Price

Black Nationalist Movements and Organizations: Up, You Mighty Race!

Since the first time that African people were held captive in the holds of slave ships and landed upon the shores of a strange and distant country, there has been a longing for freedom in independent black communities. In its most advanced form, the political, economic, and cultural organization to achieve such independence is called nationalism.

Historically, nationalism among African Americans has taken two distinct forms. There have been those who have advocated a return to the homeland of Africa, and those who have fought for the acquisition of land or the construction of independent political and social institutions here in the United States.

Those who wanted to return to Africa have claimed a desire to go where they will be adequately respected. The most concrete example of this political movement is the African country **Liberia,** founded by African American colonists of the white-run **African Colonization Society** in 1821. Liberia still exists today as an example of the many challenges involved in repatriation and colonization on the African continent.

In 1914, a young Jamaican who was living in Britain, **Marcus Garvey,** started the **United Negro Improvement Association and African Communities League** (UNIA-ACL). Hugely influenced by **Booker T. Washington's** message of self-help, his intent was to organize black people to help themselves. In 1920, Garvey held the first UNIA-ACL convention in New York, and soon the organization had 1,100 chapters across the globe and had started a worldwide shipping company that would work between the Caribbean, Africa, and America—the **Black Star Line.** Garvey's plan to sell stock in the enterprise was quite successful, but was hamstrung by poor management, and eventually dissolved when Garvey was convicted on specious charges of mail fraud in 1922.

Two members of Garvey's UNIA were Earl and Louise Little, parents of a boy named Malcolm. Malcolm later dropped his last name and adopted the surname X when he joined the **Nation of Islam** (NOI). The Nation of Islam, founded by **Elijah Muhammad** through the teachings of **Fard Muhammad** in 1934, demands territory for a separate state dedicated to people of African descent in their mission statement. **Malcolm X,** a model student turned hustler by the restrictions of race, joined the Nation of Islam while incarcerated in 1948 for armed robbery. Through incredible leadership abilities and oratorical skill, he galvanized the NOI and heightened its profile considerably—beyond the limitations set by Elijah Muhammad. Malcolm was expelled from the NOI in 1964, and Malcolm was assassinated by NOI members the next year. His *Autobiography of Malcolm X* is essential reading for those interested in the history of nationalist struggle. The Nation of Islam still survives today with **Minister Louis Farrakhan** at the helm of the organization.

Malcolm's death, combined with some of the frustrations caused by the Civil Rights Movement and the assassination of Martin Luther King, caused a resurgence in interest by young activists. The Student Non-Violent Coordinating Committee (SNCC) was an arm of the Southern Christian Leadership Council (SCLC). SNCC member **Stokely Carmichael,** who later changed his name to **Kwame Toure,** was a voter registration activist in Lowndes County, Alabama in 1965. He helped to start a political party that chose a Black Panther as a symbol to instruct the new black voters where to cast their vote on the ballot. Carmichael started the chant which was to ring throughout the black protest movement of the 60s—"Black Power." Toure later founded the **All African People's Revolutionary Party,** a Pan African organization that seeks to unite African people around the world.

In 1966, **Huey Newton** and **Bobby Seale** started the **Black Panther Party for Self Defense** (BPP), in Oakland, California. The Black Panthers quickly developed chapters across the United States, creating free food, medicine, educational programs, and self-defense training for black men and women. The **Black Panther Party Ten Point Program** was as follows:

1. We want freedom. We want power to determine the destiny of our Black Community.

2. We want full employment for our people.
3. We want an end to the robbery by the white man of our Black Community.
4. We want decent housing, fit for shelter of human beings.
5. We want education for our people that exposes the true nature of this decadent American society. We want education that teaches us our true history and our role in the present-day society.
6. We want all black men to be exempt from military service.
7. We want an immediate end to police brutality and murder of black people.
8. We want freedom for all black men held in federal, state, county and city prisons and jails.
9. We want all black people when brought to trial to be tried in court by a jury of their peer group or people from their black communities, as defined by the Constitution of the United States.
10. We want land, bread, housing, education, clothing, justice and peace. And as our major political objective, a United Nations-supervised plebiscite to be held throughout the black colony in which only black colonial subjects will be allowed to participate for the purpose of determining the will of black people as to their national destiny.

The BPP were subject to harassment and intimidation by the FBI's COINTELPRO spy program, and many members were jailed and co-erced until the organization was effectively dispersed by the late 70s.

Another group, the **Republic of New Afrika** (RNA), was founded in Detroit, Michigan in 1968. The RNA claimed the states of Louisiana, South Carolina, Mississippi, Georgia, and Alabama as black territories as reparations for slavery. They attempted to legally homestead in Mississippi but were forcefully expelled and jailed in 1972. They are still loosely organized today as the **Malcolm X Grassroots Movement.**

The quest for black independence continues today, every time black folks create organizations that are funded, managed, and controlled by themselves.

Books to check out!

Message to the People: The Course of African Philosophy by Marcus Garvey
Black Power: The Politics of Liberation in America by Stokely Carmichael
    and Charles Hamilton
The Black Power Movement edited by Muhammad Ahmad, Ernie Allen, and
    John H Bracey

The Harlem Renaissance
1922–1935

It could be argued that the Harlem Renaissance started with *The Liberator's* publication of **Claude McKay**'s poem "If We Must Die" during the riots of 1919. It is clear, however, that by the time McKay's collected works, *Harlem Shadows*, was published in 1922, the Renaissance was in full effect.

After World War I, in the midst of great social upheaval from returning veterans and the first great migration of blacks to the north, the stage was set for an upsurge in creativity among young black artists. This happened most significantly in the black heart of the nation's biggest city—Harlem, New York. There, a kind of critical mass occurred, a meeting of young, adventurous minds that combined with fledgling organizations and publications that were eager to present art and critique by new black artists and intellectuals.

The New Negro, along with *Crisis* and *Opportunity* magazines, proved to be major catalysts for this black artistic rebirth. **Jessie Fausset,** a renowned poet and author of *Plum Bun* (1926), was editor of the journal

Crisis, a publication of the **National Association for the Advancement of Colored People (NAACP)**. *Crisis* served as an anti-lynching rallying cry as well as a means for discussion of important artistic issues.

The **National Urban League** published *Opportunity* magazine, which sponsored an important literary award that was won by the likes of **Langston Hughes** and **Zora Neale Hurston.** *Opportunity* also published seminal essays such as "The Negro Artist and Modern Art" by **Romare Bearden.** In 1925, **Alain Locke,** a Howard University professor and the first black Rhodes Scholar, published *The New Negro.* This groundbreaking anthology presented writings, articles, and critique by emerging authors such as **Langston Hughes, Zora Neal Hurston, Claude McKay, Jean Toomer, Countee Cullen, Anne Spencer, Arna Bontemps,** and **Charles Johnson.** In addition, the work of visual artists **Aaron Douglass, Miguel Covarrubias** and **W.V. Ruckterschell** were featured alongside pictures of traditional African masks.

Blacks were appearing in white publications as well. Langston Hughes and **George Schuyler** both placed articles in *The Nation.* Hughes's "The Negro Artist and the Racial Mountaintop" threw down the gauntlet of a new black voice that was speaking only for itself, while Schuyler's "The Negro-Art Hokum" questioned the idea of a black aesthetic. Other achievements during the Harlem Renaissance include the addition of bibliophile **Arthur Schomburg**'s vast collection to the New York Public Library system in 1926. This occasion marked the beginnings of the world famous **Schomburg Center for Research in Black Culture.** Also, **Wallace Thurman** published *Fire!!*, an independent magazine that featured works by daring writers, such as **Richard Bruce Nugent**'s "Smoke, Lillies and Jade," an experimental prose piece that explored gender roles and drugs. While only lasting one issue, in 1926, its contributors were quite influential.

The Renaissance lasted up to the time of the **Harlem Riot of 1935,** when three lives and two million dollars of property were lost. In a little more than one decade, African American artists had shocked America with their genius.

Books to check out!

Remembering the Harlem Renaissance by Cary D. Wintz
Encyclopedia of the Harlem Renaissance by Aberjhani and Sandra West
Black Writers Interpret the Harlem Renaissance by Cary D. Wintz

The Black Arts Movement: Expressing Beauty in Blackness

From the mid-60s until the late-70s, a new generation of artists, theorists, and cultural workers labored to create a new vision of blackness. The Black Arts Movement (BAM) embodied the growing need among black folks to create poetry, art, song, and fiction that challenged the traditional views of blackness and affirmed the connection to African peoples and political struggles.

If folks wanted to be free of physical and mental oppression and in charge of themselves and their communities, it followed that they needed to create new ways of expression that would allow them to see themselves as beautiful, powerful, whole, black human beings. BAM defied the typical stereotypes of bowed, shuffling, and acquiescent negroes. Thus, one of the first words to be rescued by the Black Arts Movement was "black": "Black is Beautiful" and "Black Power" became catch phrases of the day that allowed us to embrace our natural beauty and combat the old notion that "If you're white, you're alright; if you're brown, stick around; if you're black, stay back." **Stokely Carmichael**

(aka Kwame Toure) catapulted the phrase "Black Power" into national consciousness in 1966 when he used it to rally crowds across the south during his work with the **Student Nonviolent Coordinating Committee (SNCC).**

In every state, and in practically every major city, organizations sprang up to champion BAM in poetry, dress, language, dance, and action. **Amiri Baraka,** who coined the term "Black Arts" in his seminal 1965 poem "Black Art," founded the **Black Arts Repertory Theatre/ School (BARTS)** in New York along with **Askia Toure** and **Larry Neal.** Toure's contribution to poetry books, such as *From the Pyramids to the Projects,* carved out a transformative vision of black poetry and won awards. A critical anthology of BAM writings published in New York is 1969's *Black Fire,* edited by Baraka and **Larry Neal,** poet, playwright, and one of the main BAM theorists, who wrote, "Black Art is the aesthetic and spiritual sister of the Black Power concept."

In Chicago, **Hoyt Fuller,** editor of the **Negro Digest/Black World,** started the **Organization of Black American Culture Writers Workshop (OBAC).** This workshop honed the work of poets **Sterling Plumpp, Angela Jackson,** and **Haki Madhubuti,** who established the nation's longest running black owned press, **Third World Press.** In Detroit, **Dudley Randall's Broadside Press** and **Naomi Long Madgett's Lotus Press** were manifestations of a black press with a black cultural nationalist message.

BAM was an extension of the politics of Black Nationalism, and as a result, many of its proponents have been called **Cultural Nationalists.**

Maulana Karenga, founder of the **United Slaves (US)** in Long Beach, California, was one such advocate. In 1968 he founded **Kwanzaa,** which may be the most popular and lasting institution to emerge from BAM. In Sausalito, California, the **Black World Foundation** began publication of the *Black Scholar,* a journal that served as a forum for critique of aesthetic and political questions of the time. In California's Oakland County, playwrights **Ed Bullins** and **Marvin X** helped found the **Black House,** which served as an arts center and headquarters for the Black Panther Party.

In New Orleans, Neo-Griot **Kalamu Ya Salaam** founded the **Nommo Writer's Group.** Today, Salaam is a successful poet, editor, and active chronicler of BAM literary and ideological history.

Two of the most important women writers associated with BAM, **Sonia Sanchez** and **Nikki Giovanni,** continue to be powerful forces in American literature. Sanchez's contribution to the black aesthetic that defined BAM includes poetry and plays such as *The Bronx is Next*, where she effectively challenges the black male hegemony of BAM with a female character who responds, "I don't owe no black man no explanations 'bout what I do." Giovanni's fame came initially through her electrifying New York readings of poems such as "Ego Tripping" and her volumes such as *Black Feeling, Black Talk* (1968), *Black Judgment* (1968), and *Re: Creation* (1970).

Adrienne Kennedy is an astonishing playwright who also played an important role in BAM. Her experimental play *Funnyhouse of a Negro* earned her an Obie award and solidified her reputation as a formidable voice. New York's **Barbara Ann Teer** established the National Black Theatre in Harlem. The 125th Street theatre was a theatre of evolution that brought black playwrights onto the stage. In 1971, **Abena Joan Brown** founded Chicago's ETA Creative Arts Foundation, the only African American full service cultural arts collective in Chicago and the nation.

Musically, jazz musicians and visual artists also organized themselves to embody BAM. In 1965, a group of Chicago musicians that included **Muhal Richard Abrams, Steve McCall, Malachi Favors Maghostut, Kelan Phil Cohran, Fred Anderson, Joseph Jarman,** and **Roscoe Mitchell** formed the **Association for the Advancement of Creative Musicians (AACM).** The group has been instrumental in fostering a new direction for black music for over thirty-five years, and has nurtured and showcased the talents of **Anne Ward, David Boykins, the Art Ensemble of Chicago, Anthony Braxton, Lester Bowie, Sun Ra, Ernest Dawkins, Niki Mitchell, Malachi Thompson, Harrison Bankhead, Avreeayl Ra, Steve Berry,** and others.

Black visual artists organized themselves as well. In 1967, painter **Jeff Donaldson** directed the painting of a mural, the **Wall Of Respect,** on Chicago's south side. The next year he joined **Wadsworth Jarrell** and **Barbara Jones-Hogu** to found **AfriCobra (African Commune of Bad Relevant Artists).** In 1973, **Sam Greenlee** released a film based on his best-selling book, *The Spook Who Sat By The Door,* a vivid depiction of the militaristic aims of the Black Power movement.

BAM also changed fashion considerably. **Afros** were a display of the newfound love we had for our hair. **Dashikis** were worn to embrace an African centered aesthetic. The term Negro was abandoned, and Black was embraced. Folks called each other "brother" and "sister" with new meaning.

The Black Arts Movement was an important step in our cultural consciousness that brought us closer to an understanding of our power and destiny. Its legacy is still felt today when black folk create art that reaffirms our humanity.

Books to check out!

Dudley Randall, Broadside Press, and the Black Arts Movement in Detroit, 1960–1995 by Julius E. Thompson

The Magic of JuJu: An Appreciation of the Black Arts Movement by Kalamu Ya Salaam

Visions of a Liberated Future: Black Arts Movement Writings by Larry Neal

The Womanist Movement

The movement that, in the 1980's, defined itself as *womanist* existed long before Alice Walker created the term in her collection of essays, ***In Search of Our Mothers' Gardens: Womanist Prose.*** Its roots reach back to the matriarchal societies of Africa, back to the will of black women to survive throughout slavery, and back through Sojourner Truth's fiery exposition before the 1851 Women's Right's Convention in Akron, Ohio when she said "Look at me! Look at my arm! I could have ploughed and planted, and gathered into barns, and no man could head me! And ain't I a woman?"

Womanism night be seen in Madame C.J. Walker's genius that created an empire by attending to the health of black women's hair and skin, and it would definitely find a place in the pages of Zora Neal Hurston's novels. Womanism was an integral part of the black women's club movement and found a voice in Ida B. Wells, Mary McLeod Bethune, Angela Davis, Ntozake Shange, and Rosa Parks. *The American Heritage Dictionary* defines *womanist* as: "Having or expressing a belief in or respect for women and their talents and abilities beyond the boundaries of race and class; exhibiting a feminism that is inclusive esp. of Black American culture," or, as Alice Walker put it:

> feminist of color . . . Also: A woman who loves other women, sexually and/or non-sexually. Appreciates and prefers women's culture, women's emotional flexibility (values tears as natural counterbalance of laughter), and women's strength. Sometimes loves individual men, sexually and/or non-sexually. Committed to survival and wholeness of entire people, male and female. Not a separatist, except periodically, for health. Traditionally universalist . . . Loves music. Loves dance. Loves the moon. Loves the Spirit. Loves love and food and roundness. Loves struggle. Loves the Folk. Loves herself. Regardless.

She further explained, in a 1984 interview with the *New York Times Magazine*:

> I don't choose womanism because it is "better" than feminism. . . . Since womanism means black feminism, this would be a non-sensical distinction. I choose it because I prefer the sound, the feel, the fit of it; because I cherish the spirit of the women (like Sojourner) the word calls to mind, and because I share the old ethnic-American habit of offering society a new word when the old word it is using fails to describe behavior and change that only a new word can help it more fully see.

Womanism offers a pointed critique of misogyny (the hatred of women) from within and without the black community. A womanist analysis also offers solutions to problems and strategies to confront sexual and physical abuse, heterosexism (bias against gays), and sexism in housing, health, and employment.

Part of the reason that black women have developed a womanist perspective is because of the discrimination they encountered within the Feminist movement that can be traced back to the suffrage movement, when prominent suffragists opted to leave them out of their organizing efforts.

Because womanism is a perspective that has been expressed so explicitly by so many groundbreaking authors, the following bibliography may provide a good start for those who are interested in learning more about black women's fight for equality and womanism.

A Beginning Womanist Bibliography

By Alice Walker
In Search of Our Mothers' Gardens: Womanist Prose
The Color Purple
In Love & Trouble: Stories of Black Women
The Temple of My Familiar
Possessing the Secret of Joy

By Barbara Smith
Toward a Black Feminist Criticism
Home Girls: A Black Feminist Anthology
All the Women are White, All the Blacks Are Men, But Some of Us Are Brave
     (w/ Gloria Hull and Pat Scott)

By Angela Davis
Women, Race, and Class
Women, Culture, and Politics

By Audre Lorde
Zami: A New Spelling of My Name
Sister Outsider: Essays and Speeches
The Cancer Journals

By Bell Hooks:
Ain't I a Woman?: Black Women & Feminism
Feminist Theory from Margin to Center
Talking Back, Thinking Feminist, Thinking Black
Yearning: Race, Gender, and Cultural Politics
Sisters of the Yam: Black Women and Self-Recovery

By Toni Morrison
The Bluest Eye
Sula
Song of Solomon
Tar Baby
Beloved
Jazz

Wild Women Don't Wear No Blues: Black Women Writers on Love, Men, and Sex by Marita Goldin

The Black Woman: An Anthology by Toni Cade Bambara.

Black Macho and the Myth of the Superwoman by Michelle Wallace

For Colored Girls Who Have Considered Suicide/When the Rainbow is Enuf by Ntozake Shange

Sisterfire: Black Womanist Fiction and Poetry edited by Charlotte Watson Sherman

The Women of Brewster Place by Gloria Naylor

Their Eyes Were Watching God by Zora Neale Hurston

Blood, Sweat, and Tears: The Civil Rights Movement

Ever since African people were kidnapped from their homeland and brought to another shore, there has been a struggle for equal protection and privilege under the law—the struggle for civil rights. However, the term Civil Rights Movement has mostly been used to describe the period of political struggle that followed World War II, continuing up until today. This period has been marked by several modes of action that work together in order to produce results—litigation through the courts, civil action and disobedience, and passage of legislation that addressed racial bias, and consequently bias against gender, religion, and sexual orientation.

There were many African American organizations and individuals that played important roles throughout the movement, but here we will focus on a few organizations and their role from just before WWII until 1965. Those organizations are the **National Association for the Advancement of Colored People** (NAACP) and its affiliated **Legal Defense and Education Fund**, the **Southern Christian Leadership Council** (SCLC), the **Student Nonviolent Coordinating Committee** (SNCC), and the **Congress Of Racial Equality** (CORE).

The NAACP has been, since its inception in 1910, the premier black organization for civil rights. In 1935, the NAACP Director, **Walter Francis White,** recruited **Charles Houston** to serve as part-time counsel and start a legal department for the organization that would argue black folks' case for equality to the nation's highest courts. Houston, a 1923 Harvard graduate and first black editor of the Harvard Law Review, was the perfect man for the job. As dean of Howard University Law School, which was producing close to twenty-five percent of the nation's black lawyers, he was crafting lawyers that would be "social engineers and group interpreters." His protégé and assistant was none other than **Thurgood Marshall,** who drew up the charter for the NAACP Legal Defense and Educational Fund, Inc. in 1939. For organizational reasons, the LDF separated from the NAACP in 1957. The most famous LDF case is 1954's *Brown v. Board of Education*, which desegregated Central High School in Little Rock, Arkansas. It was a legal milestone for American jurisprudence that overturned the hateful *Plessy v. Ferguson* "separate but equal" doctrine. During the 1950s, LDF won many cases that barred discrimination in housing, voting access, and jury selection, and the use of forced confessions and denial of counsel. In the 60s, the LDF took forty-five of these cases to the Supreme Court, and won nearly all of them. It has been at the forefront of the effort to abolish the death penalty, and participated in every important Supreme Court case on the issue of voting rights.

Case by case, LDF lawyers have led the charge, slowly gaining legal victories for African Americans that have benefited every American in the long run. LDF lawyers like **Jack Greenberg, William Hastie, Constance Baker Motley, Marian Wright Edelman, James Nesbrit Jr., James Nabrit II, Oliver W. Hill, Spottswoood W. Robinson III, Wiley Austin Branton, Wiley Branton, William T. Coleman,** and many others fought ingenious legal battles despite, in many cases, death threats on themselves and loved ones. The organization continues to fight for equality today in the field of education, employment, and voting rights.

The NAACP has proven to be the most lasting of civil rights organizations, and continues to organize as it approaches its century mark. In the 60s, it collaborated with the SCLC and CORE in order to move masses of people into social and political action. The **Birmingham Bus Boycott** was started by **Rosa Parks,** who refused to give up her seat on a segregated bus, **E.D. Nixon,** a Pullman porter who organized the boycott, **Martin Luther King Jr.,** who evangelized the boycott into a movement, and members of the **Montgomery Improvement Association.** This seminal event provided an excellent example of the way civil disobedience, legal action, and mass organization can combine to create an undeniable political force for change. The boycott, which lasted over a year of bombings, intimidation, and lots of walking, paralyzed the city and eventually provided legal relief for the black citizens of Montgomery.

It was a template for future actions such as the **Freedom Rides,** initiated by CORE to deliberately break the law and challenge segregated facilities across the south. **George Houser, James Farmer, Anna Murray,** and **Bayard Rustin** had established CORE in 1942. Freedom Rides were also modeled on CORE's 1947 **Journey of Reconciliation,** an organized bus trip that violated Jim Crow laws of the south and drew attention to segregation. By 1961 CORE had fifty-three chapters throughout the United States. James Farmer led the organization on a series of student sit-ins that ended restaurant and lunch-counter segregation in twenty-six southern cities and several public parks, swimming pools, theaters, churches, libraries, museums, and beaches. This was dangerous work. Participants in sit-ins and freedom rides were required to restrict themselves from fighting back against kicking, hitting, spitting, and verbal abuse, and to submit to jail where they would often be tortured.

James Peck, a member of the Freedom Riders, wrote about his experiences in Alabama in 1961, in his book, *Freedom Rider*.

> When the Greyhound bus pulled into Anniston, it was immediately surrounded by an angry mob armed with iron bars. They set about the vehicle, denting the sides, breaking windows, and slashing tires. Finally, the police arrived and the bus managed to depart. But the mob pursued in cars. Within minutes, the pursuing mob was hitting the bus with iron bars. The rear window was broken and a bomb was hurled inside. All the passengers managed to escape before the bus burst into flames and was totally destroyed. Policemen, who had been standing by, belatedly came on the scene. A couple of them fired into the air. The mob dispersed and the injured were taken to a local hospital.

CORE collaborated with SNCCC and SCLC in the coordination of sit-ins and Freedom Rides. CORE, SNCC, and NAACP also established 30 **Freedom Schools** in towns throughout Mississippi, where volunteers taught black history, the philosophy of the civil rights movement, and the necessity of voting rights. Meanwhile, SNCC members such as **Bob Moses** and **Stokely Carmichael** were instrumental in establishing the 1963 **Freedom Ballot,** which quadrupled the number of registered black voters, and in founding the **Mississippi Freedom Democratic Party** (MFDP). In the summer of '64, thirty black homes and thirty-seven black churches were firebombed, and racist cops or white mobs beat over eighty volunteers. Finally, two white New Yorkers, **Andrew Goodman** and **Michael Schwerner,** and a native black Mississippian, **James Chaney,** were martyred for their political agitation. Undaunted, SNCC took the MFPD to the 1964 Democratic National convention in Atlantic City, with the goal of gaining representation for Mississippi blacks that the state's current delegation would not provide. While they did not get representation in the convention, they made great strides toward black voter representation in Mississippi.

Another seminal event, which included all the above organizations, was the **1963 March on Washington. Roy Wilkins** of the NAACP, SNCC leader **John Lewis, Phillip Randolph** of the **Brotherhood of Sleeping Car Porters, Whitney Young** of the **National Urban League,** James Farmer of CORE, and Martin Luther King Jr. of the SCLC co-chaired this march that brought 200,000 dedicated, orderly black and white marchers to Washington's Lincoln Memorial. A watershed event in black history, it marked one of the greatest moments in American oratory with King's "I Have a Dream" speech, and spurred passage of the 1964 Civil Rights Act, which outlawed racial discrimination in public facilities. The Voting Rights Act of 1965 eliminated barriers to voting such as literacy tests and poll taxes, devices that states routinely used to block black folks from the voting booth. These landmarks in legislation marked the end of legal apartheid in the United States. But it left much work to be done, as is evidenced by the many hurdles that awaited and still await those who sought and still seek equality.

The struggle for civil rights continues today in the elimination of bias along gender, race, religion, and sexual preference. Another critical part of that struggle has been the concept of affirmative action, a way to guarantee an equal distribution of contracts and jobs to minority populations traditionally underrepresented in the higher paid sectors of America's workforce.

It is impossible to cover the entire history of the civil rights movement here, as there have been so many heroes, sung and unsung, who have laid down their lives and personal freedom for the ideal of equality. It is our obligation to learn and understand as much as possible about the history of civil rights in order to safeguard them for the future.

Books to check out!

The Eyes on the Prize: Civil Rights Reader: Documents, Speeches, and First-hand Accounts from the Black Freedom Struggle, 1954–1990 by Clayborne Carson, Martin Luther King Jr., David J. Garrow (Editor), Darlene Clark Hine (Editor)

Eyes on the Prize: America's Civil Rights Years, 1954–1965 by Juan Williams

Freedom's Daughters: The Unsung Heroines of the Civil Rights Movement from 1830 to 1970 by Lynne Olson

SOCIAL/IDEOLOGICAL GROUPS

Red and Black: A Crossroads of History and Culture

The most stirring account of African Americans and Native Americans building community is the story of the Seminole community, which you can read about in more detail in this book's section on Maroon Communities. However, history is full of cooperation between the two races, both in the form of specific individuals and particular events.

Jean Baptiste Pointe DuSable, a native Caribbean, was born to a French sailor and an African slave woman in 1745. After a Parisian education, he sailed to the new American territory of Illinois in 1779. He overcame the British Government's suspicions of Frenchmen and received charge of a settlement on the St. Charles River. DuSable entered the fur trading business and purchased 800 acres of land with his new Pottawatomie wife, Catherine. Together, they hosted white and native travelers for several years as their homestead grew to include a bakehouse, dairy, poultry house, barn, and mill. At one point Jean even entered an election to be chief of the Mackinac Indian nation. They stayed at their homestead for sixteen years before moving to St. Charles,

Missouri, but their little settlement grew until it became the city of Chicago.

York was a house slave born to the Clark family of Virginia in 1780. Because some slave owners encouraged friendships of their sons to particular slaves as long as they remembered their social station, he became friends with their son, William. Clark got possession of York when his parents died in 1799. Soon after that, he got an offer from his best friend, Meriwether Lewis, to join an expedition into the newly purchased Louisiana Purchase. Clark agreed to come, as long as he could take York. York became an ambassador and backwoodsman for the expedition, amazing those natives who had never seen a black man before with his color, strength, speed, and affable but fierce nature. Upon return to Virginia, Clark eventually set York free along with a gift of wagon and horses, which York used to run a transportation business.

After the Lewis, Clark, and York expedition opened up western territory, a pioneer of white, native, and black heritage became well known for his daring and expertise on the western trails. **Edward Rose,** master of a dozen native languages, became a guide for the Missouri, Rocky Mountain, and American fur companies in the early 1800's. In 1809, he was one of the first non-natives to venture to Yellowstone.

Frontiersman **James Beckwourth,** mixed product of a white master and his slave in 1798, left his apprenticeship to a blacksmith when he punched him out and walked out the door. He ventured west to become an army scout (against the Seminole nation, unfortunately), gold prospector, Crow chief, and the guide through a pass in the Sierra Nevada Mountains that is now known as California's Route 70. Near the highway is the town named for him, Beckwourth, California.

One of the first world famous sculptors was of Chippewa and black ancestry. She spent her first twelve years under the name Wildfire, and attended Oberlin College under the adopted name **Edmonia Lewis.**

It is also important to recognize that of the Five Civilized Nations, only the Seminoles rejected outright the European system of slavery. The Choctaw, Chickasaw, Cherokee, and Creek nations adopted a form of slavery that, in general, was much more lenient than that of their white counterparts.

Quite a few black people have some native blood running through their veins. It is not a denial of one's African heritage to claim our native, white, or other heritage along the way.

Books to check out!

Black Warrior Chiefs, a History of the Seminole Negro Indian Scouts by Cloyde I. Brown

Black, Red, and Deadly: Black and Indian Gunfighters of the Indian Territory, 1870–1907 by Arthur Burton

Black Caribbean American Achievement: Another Shade of Black

African Americans of Caribbean descent have made considerable contributions to American political and cultural life. Here are just a few of them:

Patrick Ewing, who played for New York Knicks, Seattle Supersonics, and Orlando Magic, was born in Jamaica.

Jamaica Kincaid is a native Antiguan and award-winning author of *Annie John* and *Lucy.*

George Matthews was born in the Dominican Republic, moved to New York with his family as a child, and later played saxophone with greats such as Louis Armstrong and Billie Holiday.

Shirley Chisholm, the first black woman in the U.S. House of Representatives, is of Guyanese and Barbadian heritage.

Marcus Garvey, founder of the United Negro Improvement Association, was a native of Jamaica.

Sidney Poitier, the first black Caribbean actor to receive movie super-star status, was born in the Bahamas.

Ivan Van Sertima, author of *They Came Before Columbus: the African Presence in Ancient America,* was born in Guyana.

Edwidge Danticat, author of *Breath, Eyes, Memory,* is a native Haitian writer.

Albert Chong, internationally acclaimed photographer, is Jamaican.

Colin Powell, Secretary of State under President George Walker Bush, was born to Jamaican parents Luther and Maud Powell.

Paule Marshall, author of *Browngirl, Brownstone,* is a native of Barbados.

Kamau Brathwaite, award-winning poet and author of *Black + Blues,* is from Barbados.

Audre Lorde, award-winning author of *The Cancer Journals* and *Burst of Light,* was born in New York to parents from Grenada.

Claude McKay, significant poet of the Harlem Renaissance, was born Festus Claudius McKay in Sunny Ville, Clarendon Parish, Jamaica.

Derek Walcott, Nobel Prize-winning poet, was born at Castries, St Lucia, an isolated Caribbean island in the West Indies.

Foxy Brown, hip-hop star, is of Trinidadian and Asian heritage.

Garth Fagan, world famous choreographer and dancer, spent his first twenty years in his native Jamaica.

Kenneth Dunkley, artist and inventor, created "Thoughts," the first work of art to fully utilize the holographic medium.

Harry Belafonte, movie star and political activist, is a native Jamaican.

Jean Michel-Basquiat, the youngest artist to be featured at the Metropolitan Museum of Art, was of Haitian descent.

The Fugees, a revolutionary hip-hop group featuring Wyclef Jean, Lauryn Hill, and Pras, have Haitian roots.

Marleine Bastien, activist, social worker, songwriter living in Florida, is founder of the **Haitian Grassroots Coalition.**

Garcelle Beauvais and **Tyrone Edmond** are models and actors of Haitian descent.

Arthur Schomburg, founder of the Schomburg Museum of African American history, was from Puerto Rico, just like actor Rosie Perez.

Roberto Clemente, a native of Puerto Rico, was the National League Batting Champion four times, won twelve Gold Gloves, was selected National League MVP in 1966, and won MVP in the 1971 World Series.

Sammy Sosa, baseball player for the Chicago Cubs and the 18th player to hit 500 career homers, hails from the Dominican Republic.

Betty King, of St. Vincentian heritage, was named U.S. representative on the UN Economic and Social Council in 1997.

Eric Holder, of Barbadian heritage, is Deputy U.S. Attorney General and a nationally recognized legal expert.

Roger Bonair-Agard, National Poetry Slam Champ of 2000, is of Trinidadian heritage.

Staceyann Chin, a renowned spoken word artist of African and Asian heritage, is a resident of New York City and a Jamaican National.

The contributions of Afro-Caribbean Americans and their offspring has been felt throughout the United States, and particularly in New York, a major settling place for immigrants from all over the world. Their presence will continue to be felt as they become more and more a part of the American mainstream.

Books to check out!

Brown Girl, Brownstores by Paule Marshall
The Butterfly's Way: Voices from the Haitian Diaspora in the United States by
   Edwidge Danticat

Black Bisexual, Lesbian, Gay, and Transgender Contributions

There have been many black gay, bisexual, lesbian, or transgendered contributors to American culture. Some of them are included in the list below.

Audre Lorde, acclaimed poet and essayist, author of *Zami: A New Spelling of My Name* and *I Am Your Sister.* Along with **Barbara Smith,** she co-founded and published Kitchen Table: Women of Color Press, the first U.S. publisher for women of color.

James Baldwin, award-winning author and literary critic, author of *Another Country* and *Giovanni's Room.*

Samuel Delaney, Hugo winning science fiction author and author of *Dhalgren* and *Nova.*

Alice Walker, author of ***The Color Purple*** and *Temple of My Familiar,* is bisexual.

Marlon Riggs, Emmy and Peabody Award winning filmmaker, created *Black Is . . . Black Ain't, Color Adjustment,* and *Tongue Untied.*

Jewelle Gomez, author of The *Gilda Stories, Forty-Three Septembers,* and *Don't Explain.*

Richard Bruce Nugent was author of *Smoke, Lilies and Jade,* an experimental short story in the Harlem Renaissance journal *Fire.* It was the first published black homoerotic fiction.

Assoto Saint, poet and author of *Stations* and *Spells of a Voodoo Doll.*

E. Lynn Harris, author of *Invisible Life, Just as I Am,* and *And This Too Shall Pass,* which debuted on Blackboard at number one.

Keith Boykin, former special assistant to President Clinton, is author of Lambda Literary Award-winning book, *Respecting the Soul: Daily Reflections for Black Lesbians and Gays,* and *One More River to Cross: Black and Gay in America.*

Other important books that provide a black BLGT perspective include: **Essex Hemphill's** *Brother to Brother;* **Joseph Beam's** *In the Life;* **Colin Robinson and Terence Taylor's** *Other Countries, Black Gay Voices;* **Delroy Constant-Simms's** *Greatest Taboo;* **Catherine McKinley** and **L. Joyce Delaney's** *Afrekete: An Anthology of Black Lesbian Writings;* **Assoto Saint's** *The Road Before Us: 100 Gay Black Poets;* **John Keene's** *Annotations;* **Cathy Cohen's** *The Boundaries of Blackness: AIDS and the Breakdown of Black Politics;* **Barbara Smith's** *Home Girls: A Black Feminist Anthology;* and **B. Michael Hunters'** *Sojourner: Black Gay Voices in the Age of AIDS.*

Bill T. Jones and **Alvin Ailey** are both dancers and choreographers with significant contributions to world dance.

Bayard Rustin, the behind-the-scenes organizer of the 1963 March on Washington, was openly gay.

Ruth Ellis lived to be the oldest "out" black lesbian in the U.S. when she reached 101. An active advocate of gay rights throughout her life, she died on October 5, 2000.

Rupaul, a transvestite, talk show host, singer, and raconteur, is an international celebrity.

Cathy Cohen is Professor of Political Science and Director of the Center for the Study of Race, Politics, and Culture at the University of Chicago, and a founding board member and former cochair of the board of the **Audre Lorde Project** in New York.

Linda Villarosa, executive editor of *Essence* magazine, wrote a courageous "coming out" essay for the publication on Mother's Day of 1991, which was accompanied by a companion acceptance piece from her mother. She later served as executive editor to the magazine.

Mel Boozer became the first black person to be elected president of the Gay Activists Alliance (GAA), and the first black gay male to be nominated for vice president at the 1980 Democratic National Convention.

The sexual orientations of significant cultural figures such as **Langston Hughes, Bessie Smith,** and **Zora Neale Hurston** have been called into question by many other sources. If these people were gay, they were extremely secretive about it, to the extent that none of their partners has come forward to acknowledge such a relationship. It is also true that if these people had declared their homosexuality at the time it would have hurt or wholly destroyed their careers. Bias towards gays continues today in the black community, which has only slowly grown more accepting of "out" GLBT men and women as their brothers, sisters, aunts, nephews, uncles, cousins and friends.

Black BLGT organizations include the **National Black Lesbian and Gay Leadership Forum,** the **Unity Fellowship Church Movement,** the **National Body of the Black Men's Exchange,** and **United Lesbians of African Heritage.**

Black BLGT contributions are as varied as the vocations of that community, from police officer to clergyman and from proud parent to schoolteacher. They are another part of African American culture of which to be proud.

Books to check out!

The Road Before Us (One Hundred Gay Black Poets) by Assoto Saint

Black Like Us: A Century of Lesbian, Gay and Bisexual African American Fiction by Carbado, McBride, Weise

Black Gay Man: Essays by Robert Reid-Pharr

Does Your Mama Know?: An Anthology of Black Lesbian Coming Out Stories edited by Lisa C. Moore

Afrekete: An Anthology of Black Lesbian Writing edited by Catherine Mc-Kinley

CULTURAL INSTITUTIONS

Black Oral Tradition: Speaking Truth to Power

In traditional African societies, the griot was the carrier of history and myth, a storyteller who memorized the stories of the community. The griot would pass down the stories from generation to generation, sustaining the collective memory of the community.

In the United States, the griot tradition survived through the African American oral tradition in folk tales, jokes, and song. Joel Chandler Harris, a white southerner from a poor family, published a volume of tales, which he claimed were from black former slaves in 1881. *Uncle Remus: His Songs and Sayings* was the beginning of a series of anthologies that chronicled Harris' interpretation of a black oral tradition. His tales included characters such as the wily trickster Brer' Rabbit, who was the inspiration for the cartoon character Bugs Bunny.

Black Folklore has given us ingenious tales of wile and resilience. In 1937, **Zora Neale Hurston**'s *Tell My Horse* recorded black folktales from across the Diaspora. **John Henry, Stagolee,** and **Shine** are famous folklore figures of resistance whose tales have survived throughout the years. Most folklore has survived without attribution to a specific author, but can now be found in volumes such as *Black Folktales*. **Julius Lester** has taken special pains to record black fables in his books, as he does in *When the Beginning Began*.

Certainly, the black oral tradition owes a huge debt to the Baptist preacher, the deliverer of Sunday Sermons who promised fire and brimstone if redemption were not sought. It is the preacher's style of exhortation and exhilaration that is emulated in the tradition of toasting. The toast is a specific form of poetry that is generally constructed within a prescribed rhythm or meter. Toasts tell stories about street life in urban settings—gangsters, gamblers, and good-time women run thick throughout, and prison or the graveyard is often the character's final destination.

In the 60s, several poets breathed life into the spoken word. **The Last Poets,** a poetry group from New York City, gave new life to poetry with African drums on the album that bore their name. **Gil-Scott Heron** took his deep voice and message of liberation to the recording studio and produced poetic work that captured the liberatory spirit of the times, such as "The Revolution Will Not Be Televised" and "Whitey on the Moon." **Wanda Coleman, Amiri Baraka,** and **Nikki Giovanni** are examples of poets who recorded their work in the studio and were equally successful on the page. They have been a tremendous influence on generations of poets.

The toast and the poets of the 60s and 70s are forerunners to the most conspicuous example of oral tradition today—rap. Beginning with "Rapper's Delight" in the late 70s, Rap music has given voice to millions around the world, combining beats with unsung lyrics that capture urban pathos and struggle.

Black spoken word poets have also forged new territory in the oral tradition. For the first eight years of the National Poetry Slam, all of the national champions were black: **Patricia Smith, Pat Johnson, Regie Gibson, Boogie,** and **Roger Bonair-Ragard.** Other prominent spoken word artists include **Tracie Morris, Staceyann Chin,** and **Saul Williams.** The oral tradition lives on as long as we keep our unique stories and communities intact. Pass it on!

Books to check out!

Slam: The Competitive Art of Performance Poetry

The Spoken Word Revolution: Slam, Hip Hop & the Poetry of a New Generation by Mark Eleveld

Listen Up! Spoken Word Poetry edited by Zoe Angelsey

A Treasure of African Folklore: The Oral Literature, Traditions, Myths, Legends, Epics, Tales, Recollections, Wisdom, Sayings, and Humor of Africa by Harold Courlander

Life: The Lore and Folk Poetry of the Black Hustler edited by Dennis Wepman

Weaving Art and Resistance: Quilting

When slaves chose to escape the plantation, they were in need of direction on the long path of the **Underground Railroad.** There were no road signs along the way to freedom, but they could follow the trail of quilts along the Underground Railroad, quilts that provided guidance and directions to safety.

Sewn by slave women, the quilts were sewn with different patterns, each one signifying a different set of instructions for the traveler. While the master thought the quilts were just quaint patchwork created from cast-off materials, slaves would display quilts in their windows as a kind of visual telegraph system for runaways.

A **Monkey Wrench** pattern would tell slaves to gather their tools to get ready for escape. A **Wagon Wheel** pattern would instruct escapees to pack all that they could to load into a wagon. A **Tumbling Boxes** pattern would tell that it was time to leave the plantation. A **Bear Paw** Pattern would indicate the correct path through the mountains. Other patterns were used in order to signify safe houses, cities, and dangerous areas.

After the Civil War, quilts have continued to play an important part in the life of black communities. Once used as covert road signs, an interest in the role of quilts started to reemerge in the sixties. In 1966, the **Freedom Quilting Bee** was started in Alberta, Alabama, to raise funds for the local branch of the Southern Christian Leadership Council. It has survived into the twenty-first century to become the largest employer in Alberta. For the women of this organization, quilts have served as signposts along the way to economic liberation.

In 1985, The **Women of Color Quilter's Network** was established, an organization that fosters the tradition of quilting and nurtures contemporary quilters who are busy creating gorgeous new patterns and motifs in their quilting projects. Probably the most famous contemporary quilter is **Faith Ringgold,** a master artist, whose work has been displayed in galleries around the world, including the Guggenheim and the Metropolitan Museum of Art.

From a few scraps of cloth and some castaway thread, black artists have created a legacy of resistance and artistic brilliance that continues to serve as an inspiration to people around the globe.

Books to check out!

Hidden in Plain View: The Secret Story of Quilts and the Underground Railroad by R. Dobard and J.L. Tobin

Always There: The African-American Presence in American Quilts, 1800–1900 by Cuesta R. Benberry

Signs and Symbols: African Images in African-American Quilts by Maude Wahlman

The Black National Anthem: Lift Ev'ry Voice

James Weldon Johnson, a native of Jacksonville, Florida, born in 1871, was the son of a headwaiter and a schoolteacher. He graduated from Atlanta University in 1894, while his younger brother, **John Rosamond,** attended the New England Conservatory of Music and graduated in 1897. Both returned to Florida, James to become principal of Stanton, his mother's school. Together, the two decided to write songs. On one occasion, Johnson sat down to write a poem in commemoration of Abraham Lincoln's birthday. John set the lyrics to a tune, and on February 12, 1900, a chorus of 500 children sang the song in Stanton school for the first time. After publishing the composition, *Lift Every Voice and Sing,* both brothers didn't think much about it—but it was passed on year after year in the schools of Florida until it spread across the south. Later, James studied law, moved to New York, and became a field secretary for the National Association for the Advancement of Colored People; and his song followed him.

The NAACP adopted the song as the **Negro National Hymn** in the 1920s, and black folks have played the tune in school auditoriums, churches, stadiums, meetings, concerts, and conventions ever since. In his 1935 biography, Johnson wrote, "The lines of this song repay me in elation, almost of exquisite anguish, whenever I hear them sung by Negro children."

Lift Every Voice and Sing

Lift ev'ry voice and sing,
Till earth and heaven ring.
Ring with the harmonies of Liberty;
Let our rejoicing rise,
High as the list'ning skies,
Let it resound loud as the rolling sea.
Sing a song full of the faith that the dark past has taught us,
Sing a song full of the hope that the present has brought us;
Facing the rising sun of our new day begun,
Let us march on till victory is won.

Stony the road we trod,
Bitter the chast'ning rod,
Felt in the days when hope unborn had died;
Yet with a steady beat,
Have not our weary feet,

Come to the place for which our fathers sighed?
We have come over a way that with tears has been watered,
We have come, treading our path through the blood of the slaughtered,
Out from the gloomy past,
Till now we stand at last
Where the white gleam of our bright star is cast.

God of our weary years,
God of our silent tears,
Thou who has brought us thus far on the way;
Thou who has by Thy might,
Led us into the light,
Keep us forever in the path, we pray.
Lest our feet stray from the places, our God, where we met Thee,
Lest our hearts, drunk with the wine of the world, we forget Thee,
Shadowed beneath thy hand,
May we forever stand,
True to our God,
True to our native land.

Books to check out!

Along This Way: The Autobiography of James Weldon Johnson by James Weldon Johnson

Ya Better Ask Somebody: Black Vernacular and Africanisms in English

When African people came to the Americas, they were forced to leave all of their possessions behind; all they had with them was their skin, each other, and their memories. And, although they were not allowed to use it, they still had their language. While they were learning to speak English in a strange and brutal land, they were also transforming English, creating words and phrases that would eventually become part of standard English. Many of the words would be regarded as slang, but just as many would become part of American speech patterns.

Zora Neal Hurston wrote a dictionary of Harlem slang in the 1930s, and many of the terms she listed then are still in use in mainstream culture. Are you *hip* to the meaning of *blowing your top* and *beating your gums*? Did you ever *catch the first thing smoking* out of town to get to the *gut-bucket jook joint* and *knock yourself out* with a *rug cutter* on the dance floor? *Solid.* Don't mind me, *I'm crackin' but I'm fackin'* about the *old-school* terms that *get faded* into *new-school* ways. But now we bout to get a little more egg-headed about it, you *dig*?

For many years, white linguists hypothesized that blacks simply mispronounced English. One of the first to refute this claim and document the influence of African languages on English was **Lorenzo Dow Turner.** Turner was a former baseball player with the Negro Leagues who went on to get a doctorate at the University of Chicago. While teaching at South Carolina State University, he noticed the Gullah speech patterns of some of his students, and started to trace their origins back to Africa. His scholarship refuted the white linguists and affirmed America's debt to African languages.

When we talk about jazz, we are using a word that originated from the Bantu, *jaja*, which means to cause to dance. When we talk about making a booboo, we are using a derivative of the Bantu word *mbubu*, a stupid, blundering way of acting. The banjo is based on an African stringed instrument whose name has roots in the Bantu *mbanza*. This fact was widely known up until white folks made minstrel shows using banjos to ridicule blacks, and black folks moved away from the banjo in shame.

And when we play boogie-woogie on the piano and get up to dance with no shame? In Bantu, we would *mbuki-mvuki*; take off in flight and shuck off anything that slows down our performance—and in Sierra Leone, to *bogi* means to dance.

When George Washington Carver worked with peanuts, or goobers, he might not have known that an African name for the plant is *nguba*. If you yackety-yack all the time, you would indulge in *yakula-yakula* on the west coast of Africa. If you think everything is okay, in Mandingo or Dogon, you would also be saying "Yes!"

There are also scores of towns in Alabama, Georgia, Florida, Mississippi, North and South Carolina, and Virginia with names that are derived from African languages. Pinder Town, South Carolina preserves the Kongo for peanut, *mpinda*. Alabama is home to Africatown, a settlement started by freed African captives who were fresh off the boat from the coast of Guinea. Chumukla, Florida can trace the origins of its name to the Bantu word for leaving, getting out, moving on to another place: *tshiumukila*. This would be quite appropriate for runaway slaves that were seeking refuge in the Florida swampland.

James Baldwin described our passion for transforming English as "this passion, this skill, this incredible music." It is our music that has slowly woven itself into the mouths of every American.

Books to check out!

Africanisms in the Gullah Dialect by Lorenzo Dow Turner

FAITH

The Black Church

The Christian tradition in the black community has consistently been the bedrock for social and political change. From the organization of the African Methodist Episcopal Church to the activism of Martin Luther King Jr., black Christians have been at the forefront of community service throughout this nation's history. In many southern territories or plantations where slaves were forbidden to gather in large numbers for fear of revolt, the black church was an "invisible institution," struggling for survival. Meeting covertly in "hush harbors," in forests or caves, slaves were able to find spiritual sustenance, and sometimes, guidance for escape.

The AME Church

In 1787, white members of Philadelphia's St. George's Methodist Episcopalian Church relegated black members to the gallery to watch services. As a result, **Richard Allen** led blacks to form their own **Free**

African Society. In 1816, he called together five other churches at a General Convention in Philadelphia and formed the **African Methodist Episcopal Church,** and served as the first Bishop. **William Paul Quinn,** the fourth Bishop of the church, organized the "Western Mission" and expanded the AME into Missouri and Kentucky. **Daniel Alexander Payne,** the sixth AME Bishop, founded Wilberforce University in 1856, and wrote the definitive history of the church's first 75 years, *History of the AME Church.* Former Atlanta congressional representative **Henry M. Turner** was Bishop of the AME in 1880, and was fearless in his struggle for civil rights until his death in 1915. **Sarah Hatcher Duncan** is another prominent voice in AME history. President of the Women's home and Foreign Missionary Society, her battles against sexism in the AME paved the road for **Vashti Murphy McKenzie** to be elected the first woman AME Bishop in 2000. Today, AME is the largest centrally organized denomination of blacks in the United States.

The AME church was composed largely of northern blacks before the Civil War who emphasized literacy and the ability to read the Bible over many of the more oral traditions of southern blacks, who had been restricted in their ability to learn how to read and write.

The very first black Baptist church to be established in America was the **African Baptist Church** in Savannah, Georgia. **George Liele,** a freed black southern Baptist who was licensed to preach to slaves on southern plantations, baptized Andrew Bryan and David George, who founded African Baptist Church in a barn in 1788. In 1794, Bryan moved his congregation to a frame building, and christened it the **Bryan Street**

African Baptist Church. Their congregation grew over the years, and resulted in the Second and Third Baptist Churches.

After the Civil War, black churches flourished throughout the South, providing the major means of social and political uplift, and an anchor for black families in a time of change and crisis, particularly with the end of Reconstruction. In 1895, the Foreign Mission Baptist Convention, the American National Baptist Convention, and the Baptist National Educational Convention produced the **National Baptist Convention.** A schism in 1915 resulted in the formation of the **National Baptist Convention, U.S.A., Inc.,** and the **National Baptist Convention of America.**

After World War I, the great migration of African Americans from the south provided an opportunity for change in the texture of northern black churches. **J.C. Austin,** born in Buckingham County in 1878, had received a Doctorate in Divinity from Virginia Seminary and served at Ebenezer Baptist Church from 1915 to 1926. During this time, he had become instrumental in the hierarchy of the NBC, USA Inc. By the time he moved to Chicago to pastor **Pilgrim Baptist Church,** he was an established preacher who was willing and able to accommodate the influx of southern migrants by wooing a former bluesman, Thomas Dorsey, to his church to initiate the spread of Gospel music as a powerful tool for recruiting new worshippers.

One of the outstanding examples of black liberation theology was **Rev. Martin Luther King Jr.,** spokesperson and practitioner of non-violent protest in the 1950s and 60s. His eloquence and tenacity helped galvanize thousands of protesters across the country. He would not have been able to do so without the tradition of preaching that he inherited from his father at **Ebenezer Baptist Church** in Atlanta, Georgia.

In 1961 a dispute within the National Baptist Convention, U.S.A., Inc., resulted in the establishment of a third organization, the **Progressive National Baptist Convention, Inc.,** with about 500,000 members. Today, the **National Baptist Convention of America** has over 2,500,000 members in 11,000 congregations, while NBC, USA Inc. has a membership of about 7,000,000 in 30,000 congregations. Clearly, these are the largest black organizations in the U.S., making them extremely important to the daily fabric of African Americans.

While black men have often served as the preacher, the backbone of the church, its main membership, has generally been comprised of women. Without the women that fulfill various duties of the church, the success of the institution would be negligible. Today, more women are stepping into the role of preacher traditionally held by men. In 1984, **Leontine Kelly** became the first black woman bishop of the United Methodist Church. The Christian church will always play an incredibly important role in the development of black communities. It is impossible to overstate the impact these religious institutions have had on America's history. The history of the black church in America is fascinating, and this author encourages you to seek out other resources on the subject.

Books to check out!

African American Religion: Interpretive Essays in History and Culture by Tim
  Fulop and Albert Raboteau
Negro Church in America by E. Franklin Frazier
Encyclopedia of African and African-American Religions edited by Stephen
  D. Glazier

Black Muslims in America

The most influential black Muslim organization in America is the **Nation of Islam,** founded by Ward Muhammad, built by Elijah Muhammad, widely popularized by Malcolm X in the late 50s and early 60s, and led by Minister Louis Farrakhan throughout the 70s and into the 21st century. Throughout the NOI's history, they have been instrumental in the transformation of thousands of black men and women from the machinations of the street to roles as productive members of society.

According to the theology and history of the organization, Master W. Fard Muhammad appeared in Detroit Michigan on July 4, 1930, and started a temple of Islam. In 1931, Elijah Poole heard about the temple from his wife and joined the congregation. He was later promoted to the position of "Supreme Minister" and his name was changed to Muhammad while he studied under Fard Muhammad for three-and-a-half years. Elijah Muhammad established elementary schools for the temple and published a newspaper, "The Final Call to Islam," in 1934. The

Michigan Board of Education harassed the school into closing, and required Elijah to enroll the students under white Christian teachers at local schools. He refused to do so, and left for Chicago in 1934, the same year that Fard Muhammad departed and charged Elijah with the development of the temple. Elijah Muhammad continued to build the temple, and used the organization's newspaper to spread his political analysis as well as a ten-point program entitled *What the Muslims Want*. In 1935, he went to Washington, D.C. to study and build a mosque and study more about Islam, and was arrested while there as a conscientious objector to military service during World War II. He returned to Chicago after the war, and continued to build the NOI, recruiting Malcolm Little, the fiery organizer and orator that was renamed **Malcolm X,** and a violinist named Louis Walcott, who later changed his name to **Louis Farrakhan.** After increased FBI/CIA surveillance due to NOI's growing popularity, and increasing conflict between Malcolm X and Elijah, Malcolm was assassinated in 1965, an event that marked a time of severe trauma for the Nation. The Nation survived, however, until Elijah's death on February 25, 1975.

Wallace Deen Muhammad, his son, was the successor of the Nation of Islam, which had grown into a national institution with a bank, a modern publishing facility, an airplane, import businesses, orchards, dairies, refrigerated trucks, farmland, and other assets in the tens of millions of dollars. Wallace, who changed his name to Warith, and his title from "minister" to "Imam," declared changes in the NOI's ideology as well. He ended the exclusion of white Muslims from the nation, and challenged the divinity of Fard Muhammad, Elijah Muhammad's teacher. This caused a split among members of the NOI, and several factions were created, the most powerful being that led by Louis Farrakhan, who left Imam Warith Deen Muhammad's World Community of Islam to establish the Lost-Found Nation of Islam in the Wilderness of North America, in 1977. In 1979, Farrakhan developed *The Final Call*, an internationally circulated newspaper that follows in the line of Elijah's *Muhammad Speaks*. Farrakhan's leadership during the close of the twentieth century and the beginning of the twenty-first is, like that of his teacher's during earlier years, undeniable. Along with the construction of the Mosque Maryam on Chicago's south side, his leadership in the Million Man March in 1995 marked the NOI's important role in the psyche and political landscape of black America.

There are many black Muslims who are not associated with either of the above organizations, who worship in temples across America and carry their faith with them wherever they go. They are all an important part of African American pride.

Books to check out!

Message to the Blackman In America by Elijah Muhammad
The Farrakhan Factor: African American Writers on Leadership, Nationhood, and Minister Louis Farrakhan edited by Amy Alexander
In the Name of Elijah Muhammad: Louis Farrakhan and the Nation of Islam by Mattias Gardell

INDEPENDENT
INSTITUTIONS

Kwanzaa: Seven Principles of Life

Kwanzaa is a celebration of community and self for black folk. It is a time when the black community remembers and remarks upon the best of ideals for a new year. The term Kwanzaa comes from the term "matunda ya kwanza," which means "first fruits" in Kiswahili, a West African language. Participants use Kiswahili throughout the Kwanzaa celebration in order to celebrate the black connection to African culture and history. Kwanzaa is a time of harvest, where the black community gets together and examines what it has reaped throughout the year, and what it will sow in the future.

Dr. Maulanaa Karenga, founder of a black cultural nationalist organization, the **United Slaves** (US), founded Kwanzaa in 1966. US served as a vehicle for his philosophy of **Kawaida,** a communal theory for black society. Karenga, who is now chair of the Department of Black studies at California State Long Beach, wanted to provide a cultural institution that brought black communities together with purpose and integrity. Kwanzaa extols seven principles of community building, called the **Nguzo Saba,** from December 26 to January 1 of each holiday season. The principles are remembered through the lighting of red, black, and green candles on each day of Kwanzaa. The principles are **Umoja** (Unity), **Kujichagulia** (self-determination), **Ujima** (collective work and responsibility), **Ujaama** (cooperative economics), **Nia** (purpose), **Kuumba** (creativity), and **Imani** (faith).

During the celebration, participants use traditional symbols such as the **mkeke,** a straw mat, to signify the foundation of the earth. The candleholder is called a **kinara.** It sits upon the mkeke and holds the seven candles of Kwanzaa, symbolizing the origins of our family. The seven candles are called **Mshumaa,** and represent the Nguzo Saba. **Muhindi** is an ear of corn that rests upon the mkeke, symbolizing the harvest of future generations. The **Kikombe Cha Umoja** is the unity cup, which is used to pour **libation** to ancestors. As part of African tradition, water is poured from the cup into the soil in order to share blessings with and remember those who have come before us—the names of deceased relatives and historical figures are proclaimed aloud in order to invoke their spirit. **Zawadi,** or gifts, are often exchanged between those who celebrate the holiday. On December 31, a **Karamu,** or party, is held to celebrate the New Year.

Kwanzaa celebrations slowly spread throughout the country in the '70s, gained much more popularity in the '80s, and are now quite common in communities across the United States. It was born out of the need for black people to celebrate themselves and their community. It is a time for folks to look to the past for inspiration and life lessons, review a year of change and growth, and to embark upon a new year with resolve and determination. This celebration is perhaps the most lasting and significant institution to come from the Black Arts Movement, something that lives in the hearts of the people and in their resolve to keep their traditions alive.

Books to check out!

Kwanzaa: A Celebration of Family, Community and Culture by Maulana Karenga

Kawaida Theory: An African Communitarian Philosophy by Maulana Karenga

Independent Elementary and High Schools

After the Civil War, Harriet Beecher Stowe remarked on the desire of blacks for education. "They rushed not to the grog-shop but to the schoolroom—they cried out for the spelling book as bread, and pleaded for teachers as a necessity of life." America was witnessing the thirst of its newly-freed population for basic literacy.

The desire for literacy was not new to the slave population—they had tried their best to educate themselves despite the threat of the death penalty if discovered. An underground black school existed in Savannah, Georgia from 1833 to 1865. In New Orleans, a black woman named **Deveaux** started the **Pioneer School of Freedom** at huge personal risk, and continued to spread her message of literacy throughout the Civil War. In 1861, the first independent black school opened under the leadership of **Mary Peake,** a black teacher at Fortress Monroe, Virginia. By 1865, the **Freedmen's Bureau** estimated that there were at least 500 independent small schools started by blacks who were willing to teach to their newly freed community throughout the southland. The

"Sabbath" school system, which operated on weekends and during evenings, was often established in churches throughout the south, and provided an alternative to those who could not attend during the day. In Sabbath school, the nine-year-old might learn the alphabet next to the ninety-year-old, and children studied math alongside their parents.

During the twentieth century, independent black schools continued to survive, primarily because of segregation in the United States Educational system and black folks' desire to see their children educated outside of the public schools system. After the **Brown v. Board of Education** decision in 1947, the need for independent black schools seemed to subside in favor of integration into public schools. During the 60s, however, black independent schools were created to establish an afrocentric pedagogy that emphasizes the accomplishments, history, and worldview of black people.

In the 1980s and 90s a new movement began to express itself, one that is an outgrowth of the Black Arts and Civil Rights Movements of previous decades—the **Afrocentric Education** movement. **Asa Hilliard** and **Molefe Kete Asante** and **Hannibal Afrik** are educators who played a considerable role in developing and spreading the word about Afrocentric curricula. The **Council of Independent Black Institutions** was established in 1979 in order to foster schools that provide an Afrocentric education for black youth. In Chicago, **Haki** and **Safisha Madhubuti** founded the **Institute for Positive Education** in 1972, one of many independent black schools that educate youth today. Other black parents are determined to take their children's education into their own hands and in their own homes. The **Afrocentric Home-schoolers Association** was initiated in 1996 in order to support black parents who want to keep their children out of public and private schools.

Books to check out!

Miseducation of the Negro by Carter G. Woodson
African American Education: Race, Community, Inequality and Achievement —a Tribute to Edgar G. Epps edited by Allen, Spencer, and O'Connor
African-Centered Schooling in Theory and Practice edited by Ajirotutu, Epps, and Pollard

Independent Press: An Alternative Opinion

"Freedom of the press belongs to he who owns one." Black folks have taken this truth to heart ever since they have had the opportunity to own and operate independent presses. The first known black newspaper sold in the U.S. was the *Freedom's Journal*, a weekly whose masthead read, "Righteousness Exalteth a Nation." Launched in 1827 by New York City's **Samuel Cornish** and **John Russwurm,** the paper's intent was clear: to advocate for the abolition of slavery. Russwurm eventually ventured to Liberia to publish the *Liberia Herald*, Africa's first newspaper, and to serve as governor on the Colony of Maryland at Cape Palmas. Cornish stayed in the U.S. to edit the *Weekly Advocate*, edited by **Phillip A. Bell.** The *Advocate* is considered the second African American newspaper. Bell changed its name to the *Colored American* in 1837. The paper survived until 1842. The names of black periodicals during the time—*Freeman's Advocate, Genius of Freedom, Aliened American*—all reflected the quest for emancipation, and were primarily geared toward convincing whites of slavery's evils. *Mirror of Liberty* was a magazine published by New Yorker **David Ruggles** from 1847 to 1849. In 1848,

Pittsburgh resident **Martin R. Delany** edited and published *The Mystery*, which survived as a quarterly until 1852.

Samuel Ringgold Ward was born into a Maryland slave family in 1817, but his family escaped in 1820 and he grew up mostly in New York, where he published the *True American* and the *Impartial Citizen*. A Congregationalist minister and passionate orator, Ward followed a lecture circuit condemning slavery, selling his paper, and writing occasional articles for the *Aliened American* and the *North Star* before he died in 1866.

Willis A. Hodges and **Thomas Rensselaer** started the *Ram's Horn* in 1847, when Hodges' letter to a white newspaper was denied publication. The paper eventually secured 2,500 subscribers, at which point it carried a prospectus for the *North Star*. The *Star* was to emerge as the most famous of antebellum black papers, mostly because of its editor, **Frederick Douglass,** an escaped ex-slave, fiery orator, and abolitionist. Douglass' first editor was **Martin R. Delany,** the first black graduate of Harvard and considered by some to be the first Black Nationalist. The paper eventually was renamed *Frederick Douglass' Paper* and lasted until 1859. He went on to edit or publish *Douglass' Monthly* and *New Era*, which folded in 1875.

At the turn of the twentieth century, several papers were started that made their mark on American journalism. In 1909, **James H. Anderson** started the *Amsterdam News* in New York with a "dream in mind, $10 in his pocket, six sheets of paper and two pencils." The *Amsterdam* still exists today, as does the *Chicago Defender*, founded in 1905 by **Robert Abbot Sengstacke.**

The *Defender*, started on a card table and printed on credit, became controversial and successful when Abbot editorialized against southern segregation and rampant lynching after World War I. Abbot urged black families to come up north, and was a major catalyst for the 110,000 who moved to Chicago alone, almost tripling its black population. **John Sengstacke,** Abbot's nephew, served as publisher until his death in 1997. Sengstacke also formed the **National Newspaper Association** to aid in the development of black newspapers in 1940. The *Defender*, while no longer under black ownership, is still published today.

During the latter half of the 1900s, black newspapers could be found in most major cities, and included the *St. Louis American, Birmingham Times, Charlotte Post, Indianapolis Recorder, Philadelphia Times, Oakland Post, San Francisco Post, Richmond Post, Michigan Chronicle, Cleveland Call and Post, Atlanta Daily World, Miami Times, San Francisco Sun Reporter, New Pittsburgh Courier, Norfolk Journal and Guide,* and *The Final Call.*

Black magazines have made a significant impact as well. *Ebony Magazine* was started as the *Negro Digest* by Chicago's **John H. Johnson** in 1942, and continues to be one of the major black magazines in production today. Other members of the Johnson family of publications have been *Black World, Tan, Black Stars, Ebony Jr.,* and *Ebony International*, but probably the most successful of Ebony's kin has been *Jet*, which can be found in black barbershops everywhere.

If there is a sister to the Johnson empire, it must be *Essence* magazine, edited by **Susan L. Taylor.** *Essence* is probably the top selling black magazine on the market today. Another publication, *Black Enterprise,* is known for its shrewd financial advice. *Vibe* magazine, founded and chaired by entrepreneur and songwriter **Quincy Jones,** has become the top-selling music magazine in America.

Other important cultural publishing institutions are **Callaloo Magazine,** a literary journal started by **Charles Rowell,** and **The Black Scholar,** published since 1969 in an effort to discuss critical issues in the black community.

Detroit has provided two examples of independent publishing in Lotus Press, founded by Naomi Long Madgett, and **Broadside Press,** founded in 1965 by **Dudley Randall.** Both inspired Chicago's **Haki Madhubuti's** *Third World Press,* started in 1968. Third World has published poets such as Sterling Plumpp and Gwendolyn Brooks, as well as scholars Chancellor Williams and Julianne Malveaux. Other black book publishers include New Jersey's **Africa World Press** and Maryland's **Black Classic Press,** which is responsible for publishing several of Walter Moseley's mystery novels.

Over the past, black folks have consistently made the decision to buy their own press to help get their freedom. They have never settled for silence.

Books to check out!

The Black Press and the Struggle for Civil Rights by Carl Senna
The Black Press in the Middle West, 1865–1985 edited by Henry Lewis Suggs

Black Fraternities and Sororities:
A Family of Scholars

Since blacks started attending universities at land grant and historically black institutions at the turn of the century, they have sought the close bonds of fraternities and sororities. When rejected by white fraternities and sororities, the decision was made to go it alone—and so, the tradition of black Greek letter organizations began.

Alpha Phi Alpha Fraternity was the first of its kind, started at Cornell University in 1906. Famous Alpha men are **W.E.B. Du Bois, Martin Luther King,** and **Paul Robeson. Ethel Hegeman Lyle** founded **Alpha Kappa Alpha Sorority** with eight fellow students at Howard University in 1908. In 2003, the sorority had a membership of 170,000.

Others followed, bringing a special brand of community service to the tradition of Greek-letter organizations. **Kappa Alpha Psi** and **Omega Psi Phi** Fraternities were founded in 1911. By 1914, **Delta Sigma Theta Sorority** and **Phi Beta Sigma Fraternity** were thriving at Howard University. **Zeta Phi Beta Fraternity** joined them at Howard in 1920, and two years later **Sigma Gamma Rho** was born at Butler

University. In 1943, **Gamma Phi Delta Sorority** was co-founded by **Violet Lewis;** founder of Lewis Business College, Michigan's only designated HBCU (Historically Black Colleges and Universities). In 1963, **Iota Phi Theta Fraternity** was initiated at **Morgan State University.** Other Black Greek letter organizations include **Phi Delta Psi, Pi Psi, Zeta Phi Beta,** and **Iota Phi Lambda.**

By providing academic support and fellowship to members, these organizations have served as an important tool to keep black students in higher education. While requiring participants to maintain a respectable GPA, their fund-raising efforts have gone toward scholarships as well as other community-based efforts that serve the black community. Throughout their history, Greek letter organizations have participated in voter registration drives, mentoring activities, and after-school programs to help black youth. Also, black Greeks generally have a brother or sister they can network with in every career field imaginable. This accessibility and loyalty provides an alternative route to success for those blocked by traditional "old boy networks."

Some black collegiate organizations have fulfilled many of the same purposes outside of the Greek letter organization structure. Social fellowships such as **Swing Phi Swing** and **Groove Phi Groove** were founded in the 60s in order to provide just such an alternative. Black fraternities and sororities made a way out of no way in order to provide fellowship and support for aspiring students. It is up to us to continue the legacy of excellence and support in academia. Whether we are in a Greek letter organization or not, we can always encourage each other to achieve the highest standards in education.

Books to check out!

In Search of Sisterhood: Delta Sigma Theta and the Challenge of the Black Sorority Movemennt by Paula Giddings
History of Sigma Pi Phi: Black History by Charles Wellesley

Black Women's Club Movement

In the late nineteenth century, black women across the country organized themselves as activists to combat racism, sexism, and disenfranchisement. From 1895 until the end of World War I and the creation of black sororities, these organizations were the primary organizing tool for black women, and **Ida B. Wells** was at the center of their development.

Wells, a courageous agitator who was known for traveling around the South with a pistol under her dress and documenting the horrors of lynching, was also a tireless advocate for women's suffrage. In 1893, during a trip to England, Wells confronted Frances Willard, leader of the Women's Christian Temperance Union (WCTU), the largest suffragist organization in the U.S. Wells highlighted Willard's anti-black statements that justified lynching and the WCTU's ban on black members in southern states. Willard and several others attempted to defend themselves by smearing Wells in the national press, but the argument brought international attention to the issue, and helped spur black women to start their own national organization that could both facilitate the work of local groups and serve as a more capable alternative to white women's groups.

That same year, **Mary Church Terrell,** a multilingual graduate of Oberlin College and daughter of one of the wealthiest black families in the south, started the **National League of Colored Women (NLCW)** with a collaborator, **Fannie Barrier Williams.** Williams gave an 1893 address on "The Intellectual Progress of the Colored Women of the United States since the Emancipation Proclamation" to the World's Congress of Representative Women, and later became a noted lecturer on black women's suffrage.

In 1895, **Josephine St. Pierre Ruffin,** a founding member of Boston's **New Era Club** and financier of the first black women's newspaper, *Woman's Era*, called together black women from across the country and united thirty-six clubs from twelve states in the **National Federation of Afro-American Women (NFAW)**. The next year, at a founding meeting in Washington DC, NLCW and NFAW merged to form the **National Association of Colored Women (NACW),** with Terrell as its first president.

The NACW served as a vehicle for black women to pursue their suffragist ambitions despite the discouragement that came from many sides: black men, white men, and particularly white women. The National American Women's Suffragist Association (NAWSA), headed by Susan B. Anthony and Elizabeth Cady Stanton, adopted a policy of "expediency" in its pursuit of voting rights for women. NAWSA argued to secure the vote for white women and to exclude the black vote because black would outnumber whites in many parts of the country, particularly the south.

Nevertheless, by 1916, with a membership of over 50,000, the NACW had organized 40,000 women in a suffrage department headed by **Sarah Garnett. Victoria Earle Matthews** was a former slave and founder of the **White Rose Industrial Association,** which helped thousands of young women who had newly migrated north find jobs and establish themselves. She also collected 10,000 signatures in a petition for passage of the Blair Amendment, written to guarantee women's suffrage.

In 1924, **Mary McLeod Bethune** became president of the NACW, in addition to her accomplishment as founder of the Daytona Normal and Industrial Institute for Negro Girls (later known as **Bethune-Cookman College**) in 1904. In 1936, she went on to found the **National Council for Negro Women,** which still operates today under the leadership of Dorothy I. Height. Operating with 254 community-based sections, the group has an outreach of four million women, and has Consultative Status at the United Nations.

In 1892, **Anna Julia Cooper** wrote her book *Voices of the South, by a Black Woman of the South,* a series of essays, which powerfully put forth arguments for black higher education. In it, she said, "Teach [our girls] that there is a race with special needs which they and only they can help; that the world needs and is already asking for their trained, efficient forces." The club movement is a perfect example of the capacity for black women to teach themselves and the world about self-help and determination.

Books to check out!

When and Where I Enter: The Impact of Black Women on Race and Sex in America by Paula Giddings

Gender, Race, and Politics in the Midwest: Black Club Women in Illinois by Wanda Hendricks

Toward a Tenderer Humanity and a Nobler Womanhood: African American Women's Clubs in Turn-Of-The-Century Chicago by Anne Meis Knupfer

Historically Black Colleges and Universities (HBCUs)

The nation's oldest private historically black university is **Wilberforce University,** established by the A.M.E. Church near Xenia, Ohio, in 1856. Wilberforce was a sign of things to come. After the Civil War, there were five million black people living in the United States, with about ninety-two percent of them living in the south. Between 1865 and 1900, over 200 private black colleges and universities were founded, primarily with the help of the American Missionary Association (AMA), the Freedman's Bureau, and independent black churches. Most of them were teachers' colleges, designed to train teachers for the explosion of black elementary schools across the country. HBCUs were established at the end of the Civil War with a mandate to uplift the race. They tended to a mission that was defined by an ex-slave who became the most powerful black man in America, **Booker T. Washington.**

Booker T. Washington was an alumnus of **Hampton University,** one of the first black colleges in the nation. Founded in 1868, in Hampton Virginia as Hampton Normal and Agricultural Institute,

Washington gained admission to the school in 1872 because he impressed a teacher with his cleaning skills. She hired him as a janitor for the school, and allowed him to work for his tuition. He was such an impressive worker, student, and teacher for the school that when the school president was asked to recommend someone to head a new black college in Tuskeegee, Alabama, he recommended Washington.

Tuskeegee Institute was founded when **Lewis Adams,** a former slave, made a deal with the state's Democratic Party to deliver black votes if they dedicated land and monies for a black teachers' college. Washington arrived in 1881 and used shrewd business tactics, leadership, and hard work to turn a one-room schoolhouse into a sprawling campus that taught blacks basic literacy and agricultural skills. Washington became a sought after speaker, and in 1895 delivered a speech at the Atlanta Exposition. The speech, known as the **Atlanta Compromise,** urged blacks to stay in the south to work, and promised whites that if they "put down your bucket where you are" and worked with blacks in industry, the two races would remain "separate as the fingers of a hand" socially. Washington's analysis in the speech is critical to an understanding of the mission of HBCUs at the turn of the century and even today. "It is important and right that all privileges of the law be ours, but it is vastly more important that we be prepared for the exercise of these privileges. The opportunity to earn a dollar in the factory just now is infinitely more important than the opportunity to spend a dollar in the opera house."

Today, some of the more prominent HBCUs are **Clark Atlanta,**

Morehouse, Spelman, Howard, Grambling, Hampton, North Carolina A&T, Fisk, Chicago State, Lincoln, Jackson State, Prairie View A&M, Tougaloo, Xavier, Albany State, Wilberforce, Dillard, and Meharry Medical College. HBCU alumni include Nikki Giovanni (Fisk '67), Ed Bradley (Cheyney Univ. of Penn., '64), Nnamdi Azikwe, first President of Nigeria (Lincoln University, '30), Mary McLeod Bethune (Barber-Scotia College, 1894), Dr. Jocelyn Elders (Philander Smith, '52), John Hope Franklin (Fisk, '35), Cannonball Adderley and Althea Gibson, (Florida A&T), Alex Haley (Alcorn State, '39), Zora Neal Hurston (Morgan State, '18), and Daniel "Chappie" James (Tuskeegee, '42). Margaret Burroughs and Ed Gardner, Founder of SoftSheen Products, both attended Chicago State. Lerone Bennet, Martin Luther King Jr., and Spike Lee attended Morehouse. David Dinkins, Thurgood Marshall, and Amiri Baraka all attended Howard University.

HBCUs were born out of the need for black students to get an education in a segregated society. They survive today because they offer a unique and personable setting where black students can advance their careers. They continue to be another reason to be proud of African American heritage.

Books to check out!

Historically Black Colleges and Universities: Their Place in American Higher Education edited by Julian Roebuck and Komanduri S. Murty
Black College Student Survival Guide by Jawanza Kunjufu

Black-Owned Businesses: Keeping It In the Black

Earl Graves, a former Green Beret captain and administrative assistant to the late Senator Robert F. Kennedy, had a vision for an independent black magazine that would be devoted to covering black-owned businesses. In 1968, he founded **Black Enterprise,** the premier African American–owned business magazine, and set a standard for reportage on black business affairs. For more than twenty-five years, Black Enterprise has posted the **"B.E. 100s"**—a listing of the largest black-owned industrial/service companies, auto dealerships, advertising agencies, banks, insurance companies, asset managers, and private equity firms in the country. In 2002, the revenue from the B.E. 100s was 2.9 billion dollars.

Houston's **CAMAC,** a black-owned energy exchange and development concern, has over 1,000 employees across the world. CAMAC made over a billion dollars' profit in 2002. Car dealers make up forty percent of the "B.E. 100s," and the most successful of them is the team of **Anthony Marc** and **Ernest Hodge** in Hartford, Connecticut, who pulled in over 427 million in profits in 2002. Boston's **One United Bank** has almost 500 million dollars in assets, and **Fairview Capital Partners, Inc.** managed 850 million dollars. The Southfield, Michigan advertising company, **Globalhue,** had over 350 million dollars in billings in 2002.

On Wall Street, black entrepreneurs are making strides as well. **Ron Blaylock,** a 1989 graduate of the Stern School of Business, founded **Blaylock & Partners,** LP in 1993. His firm has comanaged four of the largest IPOs—Travelers Property Casualty Corp., Prudential Financial, Inc., Kraft Foods Inc., and Agere Systems Inc.

Detroit's **Suzanne Shank,** founder and CEO of Siebert Brandford Shank & Co., helped arrange financing for the Lions' and Tigers' new stadiums, the Detroit Public School renovations, and the Detroit/Wayne County Metropolitan Airport's midfield terminal. Her firm is ranked sixteenth nationally and she was senior manager of $3 billion of public finance deals in 2001.

Betty J. Price was a sixteen-year old high school dropout with two kids. She went on to get three advanced degrees from California universities, taught mathematics for twenty years in the public schools, and served on several boards. She also founded **Kola Nut Travel, Inc.,** and now coordinates the annual **African American Women in Business Conference.** Betty is unique, but there are many other black women like her. According to the 2002 U.S. Department of Commerce statistics, black women own 365,110 firms and represent thirty percent of all businesses owned by women of color in America.

One of Shank's predecessors was the very first female bank president, Virginia's **Maggie Lena Walker.** Walker organized the **St. Luke's Penny Savings Bank,** intended to be a repository for the funds of the **Independent Order of St. Luke,** an insurance company founded in 1867 by a former slave, **Mary Prout.** Both ventures were extremely successful for their time, with 650 branches in fourteen states.

In 1899, an ex-slave, **John Merrick,** invested the profits from his chain of barbershops into banking. He joined forces with **Dr. A.M. Moore** and **Robert Fitzgerald,** owner of Durham, North Carolina's largest brickyard, and hired **Charles Spaulding** as general manager. Today, **North Carolina Mutual Life Insurance Company** has 213 million dollars in assets, and is the biggest black owned insurance company. The determination of black folks to start their own businesses and make them successful has always been a driving force for our people. The future of black-owned businesses is the future of African Americans.

Books to check out!

Black Enterprise Magazine
The History of Black Business in America by Juliet E. K. Walker
The New Color of Success: Twenty Young Black Millionaires Tell You How They're Making It by Niki Mitchell

BLACK POLITICS

Notable Blacks in Congress: Laying Down the Law

After the Civil War, The U.S. entered a period called Reconstruction, during which radical changes in electoral law took place. African Americans were allowed to run for office, and were able to win elections because of the heavy black population in the southern states. This period lasted from 1867 to 1877, when President Rutherford B. Hayes agreed to a compromise that withdrew Union troops from the South.

It is estimated that over 1,400 southern blacks held publicly elected positions during Reconstruction. Many of these folks were former slaves and runaway slaves who had come back to the South. They were craftsmen, carpenters, barbers, ministers, masons, teachers, storekeepers, and mechanics who were elected into positions of power over white and black citizens. They served as sheriffs, clerks, treasurers, tax collectors, judges, and harbor masters. Because many white people hated the idea of black political power, these office holders were maligned and their efforts often undermined by opponents.

The first African-American senator was **Hiram Revels.** Campaigning in Natchez, Mississippi, Revels was elected Alderman in 1868 and state senator from Adams County in 1869. In 1870, he won a hotly contested election to become the first African-American member of the United States Senate. Ironically, Revels was elected to fill the position vacated by Jefferson Davis almost ten years earlier (when he became the President of the Confederate States of America). Revels took his seat in the Senate on February 25, 1870 and served through March 4, 1871, the remainder of Davis' vacated term. As a member of the Committee on the District of Columbia and the Committee on Education and Labor, he voted against segregation in Washington D.C. public schools. After serving his term, he became president of Alcorn State College, the first black land-grant college.

Blanche K. Bruce, a wealthy black plantation owner, won a Mississippi election and became the first black senator to serve a full term—from 1875 to 1881. He later was register of the U.S. Treasury and trustee on the board of Howard University.

The first black member of the U.S. House of Representatives was **Joseph Hayne Rainey,** a former South Carolina slave. Rainey was elected to the state senate in 1870, where he chaired the Finance Committee. He then ran in a special election to represent the First District of South Carolina in the U.S. House of Representatives. On December 12, 1870, he was sworn in as a Member of the Forty-first Congress. During his tenure, he joined the Committee on Freedmen's Affairs, the Indian Affairs Committee, and the Committee for a Proposed National Census of 1875. He served through the Forty-fifth Congress and was unseated in 1878.

There were thirteen other blacks elected to the U.S. House of

Representatives during Reconstruction, including Jeremiah Haralson, Ala.; James T. Rapier, Ala.; and Benjamin S. Turner, Ala.; Jefferson Long, Ga.; Charles Nash, La.; John Lynch, Miss.; Richard H. Cain, Robert DeLarge, Robert Elliot, Alonzo Ransier, and Robert Smalls all represented South Carolina.

After the 1877 Compromise, no African Americans served as senator for eighty-six years. In 1928, Illinois' **Oscar DePriest** became the twentieth century's first African American to win a seat in the U.S. House of Representatives. He was the only black in Congress until 1935, and successfully proposed and pushed for passage of a bill barring discrimination in the Civilian Conservation Corps. In 1967, **Edward W. Brooke** became the first black senator in the twentieth century. He represented Massachusetts until 1979, and along the way became the first senator to call for Nixon's resignation for his involvement in the Watergate scandal and advocated a boycott of South Africa because of its apartheid policy.

In 1993, **Carol Moseley-Braun** became the first African American woman in the country, and the first woman representative of Illinois to be elected Senator. After earning a law degree from University of Chicago in 1972, she worked for the Illinois State Attorney's office. In 1978, she was elected to the Illinois state legislature, and was eventually named Assistant Majority Leader. She served one term as Recorder of Deeds for Cook County before running for the United States Senate, where she served for one term. She was later appointed U.S. Ambassador to New Zealand.

107 African Americans had been sworn in as representatives or senators by the time of the 107th Congress in 2002. Other notable black legislators have included **Adam Clayton Powell** and **Shirley Chisholm.** Powell, a former minister and business manager of the Abyssinian Church, was elected as an independent to the New York City Council, and was elected to Congress in 1944. He became chairperson of Committee on Education and Labor and attended the 1955 Bandung Conference. He served his last year in 1972.

Shirley Chisholm became the first African American woman to serve in Congress in 1968. In office, she hired an all-female staff and became a co-founder of the National Organization for Women. She ran for president in 1972, the same year that **Barbara Jordan,** in the Texas State Senate's first black legislator since 1883, was elected to U.S. House of Representatives and assigned to House Judiciary Committee.

1968 was the year a record-breaking nine African American Congresspersons were elected. In 1972, they joined more colleagues and founded the **Congressional Black Caucus** in order to advocate on behalf of African American interests. They have helped to address numerous issues of equity for people of African descent on an international and national scale.

Members of the 107th Congressional Black Caucus are Sanford Bishop, Ga.; Corrine Brown, Fla.; Julia Carson, Ind.; Donna Christian-Christensen, V.I., Del.; William Clay, Mo.; Eva Clayton, N.C.; James Clyburn, S.C.; John Conyers, Mich.; Elijah Cummings, Md.; Danny Davis, Ill.; Chakka Fattah, Pa.; Harold Ford, Jr., Tenn.; Alcee Hastings,

Fla.; Earl Hilliard, Ala.; Jesse Jackson, Jr., Ill.; Sheila Jackson-Lee, Tex.; Stephanie Tubbs Jones, Ohio; William Jefferson, La.; Eddie Bernice Johnson, Tex.; Carolyn Kilpatrick, Mich.; Barbara Lee, Calif.; John Lewis, Ga.; Cynthia McKinney, Ga.; Carrie Meek, Fla.; Gregory Meeks, N.Y.; Juanita Millender-McDonald, Calif.; Eleanor Holmes-Norton, D.C.; Major Owens, N.Y.; Donald Payne, N.J.; Charles Rangel, N.Y.; Bobby Rush, Ill.; Robert Scott, V.A.; Bennie Thompson, Miss.; Edolphus Towns, N.Y.; Maxine Waters, Calif.; Diane E. Watson, Calif.; Melvin Watt, N.C.; and Albert R. Wynn, Md.

Books to check out!

Black Members of the United States Congress, 1789–2001 by Mildred Amer
Black Americans in Congress, 1870–1989 by Bruce Ragsdale

Not Gone, Not Forgotten: Political Prisoners, Activists, and Martyrs

It is useful and respectful in a book such as this to recall the many African Americans that have voluntarily risked and suffered imprisonment and death because of their quest for civil and human rights. It is useful because we need to keep in mind the fact that the struggle for equality is not risk free, that it does not come without sacrifice. It is respectful to acknowledge the advances that were gained through the sacrifices of these individuals. It is instructive to study the reasons and causes of their travail in order that we may learn from their mistakes and successes.

For the purposes of this discussion, the term political prisoner refers to those who have been incarcerated as a result of their political speech or action in an attempt to silence, discredit, or destroy them. Generally, political prisoners are affiliated with a particular group or ideology that is in opposition to the political status quo. Often, they are arrested on either trumped up charges, or they have knowingly broken a law that they feel is unjust in order to achieve a goal of equality.

Martin Luther King was often jailed for his political speech and action, particularly when he used nonviolent protest to challenge unjust laws. In his "Letter from the Birmingham Jail" he said, "One has not only a legal but a moral responsibility to obey just laws. Conversely, one has a moral responsibility to disobey unjust laws. I would agree with St. Augustine that "an unjust law is no law at all." He went on to define just and unjust laws when he said, "An unjust law is a code that a numerical or power majority group compels a minority group to obey but does not make binding on itself. This is difference made legal. By the same token, a just law is a code that a majority compels a minority to follow and that it is willing to follow itself. This is sameness made legal."

Hundreds of activists in the Civil Rights Movement became willing political prisoners when they engaged in civil disobedience and broke unjust Jim Crow laws that enforced segregation and impoverished their communities' physical, mental, and spiritual resources. Those arrested for their activities include luminaries mentioned elsewhere in this book such as **Bayard Rustin, Fannie Lou Hamer, Angela Davis, Adam Clayton Powell, and Randall Robinson**. Others include **Stokely Carmichael, James Farmer, John Lewis, Bob Moses, Rosa Parks, John Lewis,** and countless more.

There are also those who have been arrested for advocating or engaging in self-defense against unwarranted police violence. Many members of the Black Panther Party for Self Defense were arrested while participating in Party programs such as free health clinics and breakfast programs for poor children.

In 1969, a 21-year-old Chicago leader, **Fred Hampton,** was taking the Black Panther Party to new heights of organization and relevance in the black community with breakfast programs, free health and sickle-cell clinics, and political education classes. His home was raided by the Chicago Police and pumped full of one hundred rounds of ammunition in the dead of night on December 4, 1969. He and Mark Clark, another party member, were killed in the raid, while his pregnant wife, **Akua Njeri** barely escaped death and later gave birth to a son, **Fred Hampton Jr.,** and both were active in the **National People's Democratic Uhuru Movement.** Fred Hampton Jr., who was later jailed for nine years on specious charges of aggravated arson in 1992, was prosecuted by a disrict attorney who had earlier declared "Fred Hampton Jr., we'll get you yet." He was freed in 2001.

In 1970, **Geronimo Pratt** was a twenty-two year old, highly decorated Vietnam veteran turned Panther leader in Los Angeles. The FBI framed him for a murder that occurred on a Santa Monica, California, tennis court while he was some 400 miles to the north, meeting with other black leaders. He spent twenty-seven years in jail, vigorously denying the charges against him against odds that would have made most people give up, before he was released in 1997 with the conviction overturned. It is important to remember that Pratt spent as much time in prison for justice as another foreign freedom fighter, **Nelson Mandela.**

George Jackson was originally jailed for a petty crime—stealing seventy dollars from a gas station—and was sentenced to "one year to life" in prison. Because of his political agitation as a representative of the Black Panther Party, his sentence was lengthened year after year, until he served ten times the minimum sentence. While incarcerated, his book *Soledad Brother: Letters from Prison* was published, making him a lightning rod of attention for the authorities. San Quentin prison guards gunned him down on August 21, 1971.

The story of political prisoners and martyrs is important to remember because it is the story of people who did not hold their own personal freedom above the collective freedom of their people. They are important to remember because they represent extreme sacrifice for a greater cause. Other political prisoners and martyrs include **Safiyah Bukhari, Massai Ehehosi, Herman Wallace, Mutulu Shakur, Sundiata Acoli, Assata Shakur (exiled in Cuba), Zayd Shakur, David Hilliard, Jalil Muntaquin, Herman Bell, Albert Washington, John Africa, Ramona Africa, Janet Africa, Michael Africa, Huey Newton, Sekou Odinga, Ruchell Magee,** and **Mumia Abu Jamal.**

The story of black political prisoners is a complex one, involving various political ideologies that have had liberation of their people foremost in mind. Political prisoners are a legacy of struggle we cannot forget.

Books to check out!

Can't Jail the Spirit edited by CEML
Hauling Up the Morning edited by Tim Blunk and Raymond Luc Levasseur.

MUSIC

Sacred Music: Spirituals and Gospel

In a very practical sense, spirituals served as black folks' liberation theology, providing a way for the enslaved to worship and escape oppression at the same time. On the plantation, spirituals such as "Steal Away" and "Sweet Canaan, that Promised Land" were used to signal safe times for slaves to run away. After slavery, the Fisk Jubilee Singers toured the nation in an effort to spread the sound of spirituals and raise money for the struggling institution. They never expected to bring home $20,000 and become ambassadors to black music after their first tour!

Gospel Music is a sacred music born from slave spirituals. It is a music with blues tunings that sprang from the southern roots of new black immigrants to the north. Many gospel singers and composers have often been blues players in their previous careers. Alabama-born **Thomas Dorsey,** originator of the term "gospel music," was once leader of Ma Rainey's Wild Cat Blues Band and an extremely successful blues composer. A religious conversion prompted him to write sacred songs, but the more conservative northern-born black congregations of his adopted city, Chicago, were initially wary of his blues-tinged songs of worship. Eventually, he was able to convince **Reverend Frye** of **Ebenezer Baptist Church** to play his songs. When Dorsey became choir director for the church, his music provided a newfound voice for the many new black southern immigrants to the north. Dorsey authored over one thousand songs, including *Precious Lord, Take My Hand,* which was written after the death of his wife and child. He is considered the father of gospel music.

Born in 1932, **Rev. James Cleveland** first sang gospel in Dorsey's choir, and later was responsible for the hits "Ol' Time Religion" and "The Solid Rock." Cleveland started the **Gospel Music Workshop of America,** which was a training ground for **Kirk Franklin, Jessy Dixon, John P. Kee,** and **Aretha Franklin,** and has over 30,000 members with 150 chapters around the world.

Mahalia Jackson is widely considered to be the Queen Mother of Gospel. Born in 1911 in New Orleans, she moved to Chicago at the age of sixteen and eventually started touring with Dorsey. Together, they popularized over 400 songs, one of her most famous being "Move On Up A Little Higher," which sold over a million copies in 1940. Jackson sang at the 1964 March on Washington, and sang "Precious Lord" at Dr. Martin Luther King Jr.'s funeral.

The world of Christian inspirational music would be unthinkable without the contributions of the **Blind Boys of Mississippi and Alabama, Albertina Walker, Lucie E. Campbell, Roberta Martin, James Cleveland, Kenneth Morris,** and **Mahalia Jackson,** to name a few. All of these artists helped shape the spirit and sound of gospel as it developed in the black church.

Many famous rhythm and blues artists came from the tradition of gospel. Aretha Franklin would not have her swing were it not for her father's preaching in a Baptist church. **Ray Charles** brought gospel stride into his popular piano playing. **Whitney Houston** learned all about singing from her mother, **Cissie Houston,** who is a famous gospel singer in her own right.

In 1968, the **Edwin Hawkins Singers** recorded "Oh Happy Day," opening the doors for the commercialization of gospel music. Today, **Andraé Crouch, the Mighty Clouds of Joy, Cece Winan,** and other black gospel artists take part in an industry that generated 920 million dollars in revenue in 2001.

Books to check out!

Gospel Music: An African-American Art Form by Joan R. Hilsman

The History of Gospel Music by Rose Blue

If You Don't Go, Don't Hinder Me: The African American Sacred Song Tradition by Bernice Johnson Reagon

Rise of Gospel Blues: The Music of Thomas Andrew Dorsey in the Urban Church by Michael W. Harris

The Blues: America's Root Music

After the Civil War, black people took the guitar and played in a way that recalled their homeland, Africa. The shiny notes from German harmonicas were bent until they sounded "blue" enough to hold a hurt that only centuries of slavery and sorrow could muster out of a soul. Thus was born the blues, a musical expression that has left its indelible mark on America.

It could be said that blues and gospel were born and raised in the same house—the plantation of the South—but that the blues parties in jook joints on Saturday night, and gospel prays in church on Sunday morning. Blues is a mixture of African musical styles conjured with European instruments and delivered in the speech and folklore of the African-American experience. It is a music that celebrates the black cat bones and mojo hands of hoodoo, an African American expression of Congolese spirituality that rivals the intensity of Christian spirituals for reverie and passion. Thus, blues was often known as "the Devil's music." As a matter of fact, **Robert Johnson,** the most famous and skilled musician to ever play the form, was said to have sold his soul to the Devil in order to play so well.

W.C. Handy, born in 1873 and a descendant of two AME (African Methodist Episcopal Church) ministers, became the "Father of the Blues" when he wrote the "St. Louis Blues" in 1914. His was the first "blues" to be published, but the first blues record to be put to wax was 1920's "The Crazy Blues" by none other than **Mamie Smith.** The "Mother of the Blues" is generally considered to be **Ma Rainey,** who sang on a southern circuit and recorded with Paramount Records in 1923. This was the same year that her protégé, **Bessie Smith,** signed with Columbia Records, where she eventually recorded scores of hits with artists such as **Fletcher Henderson** and **Louis Armstrong.**

Blues sprung out of the soil where black people tread: it is a music made unique to its surroundings. **Delta Blues** comes from the deep south of Mississippi, Alabama, and Georgia. **Chicago Blues** was formed when black folks came up north and had to amplify their instruments in order to be heard in noisy clubs. Some of the most famous practitioners of Delta Blues have been **Robert Johnson, Lightnin' Hopkins, John Lee Hooker, Howlin' Wolf,** and **Muddy Waters.** Waters and Wolf both moved to Chicago after World War II and had a friendly band rivalry for years. Waters was often accompanied by Willie Dixon, a former boxer who turned his fingers to picking the bass and churned out more than 500 blues songs, such as "Hoochie Coochie Man." These men, along with vocalists like **Koko Taylor** (who gave us the "Wang Dang Doodle") and harmonica players such as **Little Walter, Walter Horton,** and **Sonny Boy Williamson,** are arguably most responsible for the development of Chicago Blues. **B.B. King,** who has thrilled audiences for over fifty years with pearly notes from his guitar, named "Lucille," and songs like "The Thrill is Gone," is a personification of electrified Delta blues. He is a living legend along with others who are continuing the blues legacy, like **Sugar Blue, Billy Branch, Corey Harris, Keb Mo',** and **Buddy Guy.**

Piedmont Blues came out of the Carolina hills, and its most famous artists have been **Sonny Terry** and **Brownie McGhee.** Brownie, who was lame, played guitar. Sonny, who was blind, played harmonica. They combined their virtuosity for over thirty years, inspiring current artists such as **John Cephas** and **Paul Wiggins.**

Jimi Hendrix was one of the most influential guitarists of the twentieth century—his electric guitar genius still holds listeners captive over thirty years after his death in 1971. While he is popularly known as a rock guitarist, he was born and bred to the blues, and his music was so far ahead of its time that people are still trying to catch up to him today.

The irresistible power of the blues can be seen throughout American culture, and folks of all creeds and colors have been "gettin' happy" to the blues for almost a century. Famous rock groups like The Beatles, Rolling Stones (who named themselves after a Muddy Waters song), Led Zeppelin, and Van Halen owe their careers to the blues style they used in their songs. Before Hip Hop, Jazz, Rock and Roll, and Rhythm and Blues, there was the blues. It is simply impossible to trace the origins of any popular American music without running across the black hand of blues in its lineage.

Books to check out!

The Bluesman: The Musical Heritage of Black Men and Women in the Americas by Julio Finn

Blues Legacies and Black Feminism: Gertrude "Ma" Rainey, Bessie Smith and Billie Holiday by Angela Davis

Conversation with the Blues by Paul Oliver

Blues People: Negro Music in White America by LeRoi Jones

Jazz: America's Syncopated Heartbeat

The roots of Jazz lay in **Ragtime,** a syncopated music plucked from the piano and hurled into the air and onto the published page like **Scott Joplin's** "Maple Leaf Rag."

In 1913, **Jim Europe** took syncopation, a creative use of horns, and a heavy dose of futuristic vision and inspiration to make the first jazz record with the **Society Orchestra.** The music that he recorded helped spawn a revolution in American music that has been felt around the world. Jazz is born from the black aesthetic, a way of hearing the world's polyrhythm and reproducing it on snare and cymbal, a way of twisting the metallic sound of horns so that they sound more like the sultry human voice, and molding the voice into scat so that it sounds more like the brass in a horn.

It is impossible to imagine American music without jazz. **Duke Ellington, John Coltrane, Billie Holiday, Sarah Vaughn, Ella Fitzgerald, Fats Waller,** and **"Satchmo" (Louis Armstrong)** are household names across the world. Where would we be without the timeless horn of **John Coltrane** or the seething trumpet of **Miles Davis**? Would it be possible to really understand the American experience without having some acquaintance with jazz? Most historians and musicologists would say not.

Jazz has evolved into many different styles. The earliest, **Dixieland Jazz,** comes straight out of New Orleans, and thrives with fast rhythm and swinging clarinets played by **Sidney Bechet** or shining trumpets bellowed like Louis Armstrong. Armstrong was arguably the greatest of all jazz musicians, particularly before WWII. He got his "chops" with the **King Oliver's Creole Jazz Band** in the early 20s, but later started his own **Hot Five** and **Hot Seven** bands that made some of the most famous records in jazz history. Their sound embodied the spirit of the Jazz Age. By the 1930s, a new sophistication crept into jazz, one heavily influenced by the big city pulse of Chicago and New York—it was called **Swing.** Swing music saw the development of large bands like **Duke Ellington's Band** and **Count Basie's Orchestra.** Duke was responsible for such hits as "Take the A Train," "Crescendo in Blue," and "Satin Doll." Basie was the father of classics like the "One O'Clock Jump" and "Sent for You Yesterday." Basie also teamed up with a young singer named **Billie Holiday,** and the legend of Lady Day was born. Her best friend, **Lester Young** was in the band with her. **Ben Webster** also launched into this era with his sax.

The 1940s saw the rise of **Bebop** and the ascendancy of the saxophone as the preeminent instrument in jazz. Charlie Parker, also know as **"Yardbird"** Parker, was the most famous jazz musician of this era, along with **Dizzy Gillespie, Cannonball Adderley, Dexter Gordon, Sonny Rollins, Fats Navarro,** and **Charles Mingus. Miles Davis** helped usher in the age of **Cool Jazz,** but did not stop there. He pushed the music into the 60s with **Free Jazz.** Stepping into the 60s along with Davis are **John Coltrane,** who recorded the incredible mantra of "A Love Supreme," **Archie Shepp, Sun Ra, Ornette Coleman, Wes Montgomery, McCoy Tyner, Elvin Jones, Thelonius Monk, Bud Powell,** and **Anthony Braxton.**

The 70s was the time of Jazz Fusion, when Jazz and Rock combined with intensity. **Henry Threadgill** and **Steve McCall** formed **Air,** and other musicians made their marks, including **Herbie Hancock, Billy Cobham, David Murray, The Art Ensemble of Chicago,** and **James Blood Ulmer.**

The 80s featured the emergence of a new vanguard in jazz, as many of the older musicians died. **Wynton and Branford Marsalis** wield their horns across the globe today, along with contemporary artists like **Cassandra Wilson, Bobby McFerrin,** and **Courtney Pine.**

Jazz is the classical music of America, the music that adopts other ethnic sensibilities while maintaining an identity all its own. It is a form that requires an extreme amount of practice, and because of its use of improvisation, some consider it more complicated than classical music.

Blacks created jazz music out of the bosom of blues and gospel, and it has always been a hybrid music. In jazz one can find remnants and expressions of Tin Pan Alley, barrelhouse, ragtime, salsa, fusion, bebop, avant garde, and work songs. It is a music that is strummed, hollered, blown, beat, brandished, fingered, stomped, plucked, and wailed all over the world, in almost every language known to humankind. It was America's main cultural export in the twentieth century, serving as an ambassador to folks in every nook and cranny of the globe.

Jazz is another manifestation of the power of black genius that every American should revere. It is another musical gift from the black spirit that has lightened the spiritual load of the world.

Books to check out!

Introduction to Jazz History by Donald Megill
The History of Jazz by Ted Gioia

Motown: Pinnacle of the R & B Experience

Detroit, the city that produced Cadillac cars and Joe Louis, also produced one of the most singular sounds of the twentieth century—the Motown sound.

Temptations, Miracles, Supremes, Jackson 5, Tops, All Stars, Pips, Marvellettes: The Motown Who's Who reads like a list of comic-book heroes. Motown heroes spun a new groove on the dance floors and in America's romantic imagination. They provided a dynamic sound full of horns, bass, guitar, and syncopated beats that crossed racial lines when it came to the universal territory of the dance floor.

Berry Gordy had nothing but a dream and a vision when he quit his $85 per week job in the Lincoln-Mercury factory, but by 1959, he had founded one of the most successful black businesses of all time. In 1957, he had his first hit with **Jackie Wilson**'s "Reet Petite," and he knew he had to follow his dream. Gordy recorded his hit-making sessions in the basement of a house in midtown Detroit. His first bandleader was "Ivory" Joe Hunter, who brought together a world-class band that recorded songs for ten dollars apiece, seven days a week. These magicians of the music studio were percussionists Jack Ashford and Benny Benjamin, with Robert White, Joe Messina and Eddie Willis on guitar, virtuoso bassist James Jamerson and keyboardist Earl Van Dyke. They christened themselves **The Funk Brothers.**

With their unfailing sense of melody and Berry's shrewd business sense, Motown went on to record names that would become household words over the next twenty years: **Diana Ross, Marvin Gaye, Stevie Wonder, Gladys Knight, Smokey Robinson, Lionel Richie, Tammi Terrel, Martha Reeves, Michael Jackson, Debarge, the Commodores, Eddie Kendricks,** and **Teena Marie.** All of these aspiring singers and musicians ended up in Berry Gordy's office signing a contract that would lead them to stardom. They also signed up for rigorous training and quality control checks from Gordy's trademark weekly sessions, where he would sit folks around a table and play all the records produced that week to vote on the cut that they would most likely spend their last dollar on. Such was the screening one had to pass to get a tune published by Motown, and join the immortal ranks of hits like "Tracks of My Tears," "Just My Imagination," "Superstitious," "Midnight Train to Georgia," "I Want You Back," "I Heard It Through the Grapevine," "I'll Be There," and "Tears of a Clown."

Along the way, Gordy would mold and shape the artists into consummate professionals; giving tips that they needed to make the most out of their breaks and keep their career on the road. Thanks to a single person with inspiration and guts, we have enjoyed a soundtrack that will last throughout history. Motown records had such a distinctive sound that they helped to erase the common label for black recordings of the time—"race records."

Gordy sold Motown for over sixty million dollars in 1988, the same year he was inducted into the Rock and Roll Hall of Fame. Today, singers like **Brian McKnight, India.Arie,** and **Erykah Badu** continue to carry on a new Motown sound. The Motown sound had crossover appeal, giving America what it needed to survive the turbulent 60's and 70's. The little 45s and 78s gave us a voice that we could all embrace. When people around the world want to feel good about the past, to remember the hope and joy that music can bring into their lives, when they want to reminisce on the light at the end of a tunnel in turbulent times, they turn to Motown to "take them there."

Books to check out!

Motown: The Golden Years by Bill Dahl
The History of Motown by Virginia Aronson
Motown: Music, Money, Sex, and Power by Gerald Posner

Hip Hop: Urban Griots Entering a New Millenium

At the turn of the 21st century, the sound of youth is the rhythm of Hip Hop. The music, art, and dance of Hip Hop has created a new mode of communication for youth around the world.

Hip Hop was born with Caribbean roots from South Bronx imagination, turntables, spray painted murals and dance moves. Hip Hop found its voice in emcees like **Kurtis Blow, Afrika Bambaataa, Kool DJ Herc, Grand Master Flash,** and the **Sugarhill Gang.** Hip Hop is B-Boys, twisting their bodies into hieroglyphic ciphers, break dancing all over New York and the rest of the world. Hip Hop is graffiti artists applying their special brand of spray-paint beautification to empty urban walls and art gallery canvasses. Hip Hop is DJs scratching their records, searching for the break. Hip Hop is baseball caps pointed to the side, homeboys and homegirls representin' with Adidas or Nikes on their feet. Hip Hop epitomizes the art of collage, the ability of an artist to take a snippet of sound and weave it into a blanket of rhythm.

Hip Hop is a constant shape shifter, changing voices and moods from generation to generation. Each generation brings something different to its history, but as of this writing there are definitely four elements that act as the earth, wind, fire, and water of the Hip Hop universe: **Deejaying, Emceeing, Dance,** and **Graffiti.** These elements were highlighted in the first major films about the phenomenon, 1983's *Wild Style* and the follow up film, *Beat Street*. Here, we will focus mainly on the old school, the folks that started the music before it earned the title Hip Hop.

Deejaying is an art form that created an instrument out of a device meant only for playing recordings of instruments: the turntable. Turntablism is a complex craft that demands wit, ingenuity, and precision to engage in sampling, a form of sound collage that allows the DJ to mix disparate sounds together to form an alternative sonic vision. Some folks trace Deejaying back to Jamaica, where **Lee "Scratch" Perry** and **King Tubby** took ordinary records and dropped musical elements from them, creating remixes or dubs that became sound collages. By the mid 70s Jamaican immigrant **Kool DJ Herc** was innovating on turntables across New York, along with his team, the **Herculoids.** At the same time, **Afrika Bambaata, Grandmaster Flash,** and **Grand Wizard Theodore** were also starting to innovate on turntables, creating new techniques of scratching, fading, and manipulating the breakbeats of songs. Flash is particularly noteworthy for creating new equipment that is standard DJ fare today. Other DJs of the time include **Kool DJ Red Alert,** and **Kool DJ AJ.** Collectively, these folks were the forefathers of turntablism, an art that continues to develop today.

Emceeing, the art of crafting lyrics over a beat that inspires or moves a crowd, is also known as rapping or beatboxing. Emcees often use call and response with their audiences at concerts, a technique often used in the black church and the low-down jook joint. The art form stems from the African oral tradition, and some of the predecessors of rap are seen in **toasts,** an African American oral tradition that celebrates the life of the street, and Jamaican oral traditions of talking over records at parties. Other prominent poets that delivered their messages over beats include **Nikki Giovanni, The Last Poets,** and **Gil Scott Heron.** Some of the early Hip Hop emcees include **Melle Mel, Kid Creole** and **Cowboy,** who helped Grandmaster Flash rock parties in the Bronx. The earliest example of emceeing that gained national attention is the Sugar Hill Gang's 1979 release "Rapper's Delight," a fifteen-minute song that stormed the airwaves from coast to coast. Other releases included **Flash and the Furious Five's** "The Message," **Afrika Bambaata's** "Planet Rock," and **Kurtis Blow's** "Christmas Rapping" and "The Breaks." New innovators of the time were the **Cold Crush Brothers, the Funky Four +1, Spoonie Gee, the Treacherous Three, the Fearless Four, Kool Moe Dee** (who invented speed rap), and **Run-DMC** (the first hip hop stars to have a crossover hit, when they collaborated with Aerosmith on "Rock This Way"). Later on, emcees such as **Public Enemy, KRS-One, Rakim, MC Lyte,** and **Queen Latifah** brought Hip Hop into the late eighties.

Hip Hop Dance is a physical graffiti that incorporates the whole body in a sign language of moonwalking, headspins, windmills, flares, turtles, backspins, and freezes. It can be divided into several distinct categories: breakdancing, electric boogaloo, popping, and locking, and uprocking.

Breakdancing, while native to New York, is a style of dance that borrows heavily from the African dance form of capoeira, a dance and martial art derived from the Congo and practiced among slaves in the Caribbean and Brazil. It originated from dancers who tried to dance within the break of a record to entertain the crowd. Some of the earlier B-Boys were **Jojo, Bom5, Crazy Legs,** and the **Rock Steady Crew.**

Uprocking, a form that originated from Brooklyn, is a "dance" which uses the entire song that is played. It was originated by Rubber Band and the Dynasty Rockers in the mid 70s to provide an alternative to fighting amongst gangs.

In California, **Don Campbell** started a group called **"The Lockers,"** the most famous participant being **Fred "Rerun" Berry,** who appeared on the "What's Happening?" TV show. Locking is an integral part of Hip Hop dance. **Pistol Pete** and his brothers started the **Electric Boogaloo** in California. The style combined locking, The Robot, and mime to dazzle audiences. Pete later starred in "Breaking," a film that showcased his dance style and talent.

Graffiti is another stunning visual element of Hip Hop. In the 70s, early innovators began tagging public and private property with their names and images in bright, colorful spray-paint and markers. Some called it defacement, but to the practitioners of this art form, they were creating an urban beautification program, an underground drum of visual images for which they would risk their lives and develop arrest records.

Some of the early pioneers were known only by their tags; **Pistol, Blade, Phase, Tracy 168,** and the **3 Yard Boys** "bombed" their work all over New York. The fad caught on and became more serious in the late 70s, and **Fab 5 Freddy** started introducing his work to New York's downtown galleries. Other graffiti artists and crews like **Crash, FBA, and Kings Arrive** sprang up in New York, and eventually graffiti art became respected and displayed in galleries and neighborhoods around the world.

If there is a fifth element of Hip Hop, it is creativity, a creativity that allowed black people to turn record players into instruments, bare walls into beautiful canvasses, robotic moves into hypnotic dance, and the rhythm of language into rap.

Who knows where Hip Hop will go in the future? It will go wherever the youth feel it, whichever way their internal rhythm bounces. Hip Hop is black people's gift to the world, a gift that people practice from Hong Kong to Iceland to Britain to Russia and everywhere else on the globe. It is an art form under constant construction and revision. Another reason to be proud of blackness.

Books to check out!

Yes, Yes Ya'll: The Experience Music Project Oral History of Hip-Hop's First Decade by Jim Fricke and Charlie Ahearn

The Last Black Mecca: Hip Hop by Robert "Scoop" Jackson

Black Noise: Rap Music and Black Culture in Contemporary America by Tricia Rose

Bring The Noise: A Guide to Rap Music and Hip-Hop Culture by Havelock Nelson and Michael Gonzalez

Classical Composers, Musicians and Singers

The United States has a long history of African American classical musicians. Kathleen Battle and Leontyne Price have had marvelous careers in the latter half of the 1900's.

Leontyne Price, who was born in 1927 in Laurel, Mississippi, sang in a Broadway production of Porgy and Bess, and later became the first black woman to sing opera on television when she appeared in a 1955 NBC production of Tosca. Her operatic stage debut did not take place until 1957, at the San Francisco Opera, where she sang each year until 1960. In 1961, she appeared at New York's Metropolitan Opera in the difficult role of Leonora in *Il Trovatore*. After a brilliant performance, she became one of the Met's leading sopranos. She won several Grammy awards for her work and retired in 1985.

Portsmouth, Ohio native and lyric soprano **Kathleen Battle** is a five-time Grammy award winner. She is the recipient of six honorary doctorates from American universities and was inducted into the NAACP Image Hall of Fame in 1999.

Both Price and Battle owe a debt to some of the singers that came before them and paved a way for them to take their bows on stage.

Elizabeth Taylor Greenfield, who was known as the "Black Swan" by her fans, was born a slave around 1817 in Natchez, Mississippi. Her mistress moved to Philadelphia and joined the Society of Friends, whereupon she freed her slaves. Elizabeth stayed with her, adopting her last name. She continued to cultivate her voice, and in 1851, gave her first public concert in New York. A testimonial concert in Buffalo raised enough funds to finance Elizabeth's trip to Europe for additional training. Her 27-note range was hailed as astonishing. The Duchess of Sutherland noticed and became her patroness, enabling her to tour cities in America and back to England in 1854 where she sang for Queen Victoria. Not only a great singer, she taught herself how to play the guitar and the harp, and was very skilled and adept at them both.

Marie Selika, was born in Natchez, Mississippi. Selika toured Europe singing for several crowned heads of state. She was the earliest black artist to present a program at the White House, for Rutherford B. Hayes.

In 1892, at the age of twenty-three, **Madame Sissieretta Jones** was the first black woman to sing at Carnegie Hall. She sang for the Prince of Wales, and was invited to the White House to sing before three different presidents, including Benjamin Harrison in 1882.

Flora Batson, a Washington D.C. native born in 1863, was known as the "Double Voiced Queen of Song." . Traveling with black bassist Gerard Miller, she performed all over the U.S. and Great Britain, China, the Samoan Islands, New Zealand, Australia, India, Fiji, and Japan.

Carol Brice, a versatile contralto from Sedalia, North Carolina, attended the Juilliard School in New York and performed with Bill "Bojangles" Robinson in "The Hot Mikado." She won a Grammy Award for her recording of Porgy and Bess, and in 1943 became the first African-American musician to win the Walter Naumburg Award.

Lyric Soprano **Lillian Evanti** was born in 1890 in Washington, D.C. In 1932, she gave a recital at D.C.'s Belasco Theater and two years later gave a command performance at the White House for President and Mrs. Franklin D. Roosevelt. In 1941, she collaborated with **Mary Cardwell Dawson** to establish the **National Negro Opera Company** in Pittsburgh, Pennsylvania, providing a venue for black opera singers to perform and study until 1962.

Classical pianist **Phillippa Duke Schuyler,** the daughter of black critic George Schuyler, was a child prodigy. By age eleven she was touring and had more than one hundred piano compositions to her credit by the time she was thirteen. At the New York World's Fair, New York Mayor Fiorello LaGuardia declared June 19, 1940, "Philippa Duke Schuyler Day." She played concerts around the world until her untimely death in a Saigon helicopter accident.

Natalie Hinderas was another child prodigy, a concert pianist at the age of twelve who became one of Philadelphia's most accomplished classical artists. This Oberlin, Ohio native was a recipient of a Martha Baird Rockefeller fellowship and an honorary doctorate degree from Swarthmore College. She was also the first black to perform a subscription concert with the Philadelphia Orchestra in 1971. Throughout her career, she promoted and recorded works by black performers and composers, among them R. Nathaniel Dett, William Grant Still, John W. Work, and George Walker.

R. Nathaniel Dett, born in 1882, graduated from Oberlin Conservatory in 1908; he then continued his education at several institutions, including Harvard and Columbia Universities. At Harvard he won prizes for his choral compositions and for his essay, "The Emancipation of Negro Music." He also studied with Nadia Boulanger in France in 1929. From 1913–1931 he developed the Hampton Institute Choir into a superior organization that won critical acclaim on tours in the USA and Europe.

William Grant Still became the first African American composer to have a symphony performed by an American orchestra. His *Afro-American Symphony* was premiered by the Eastman Rochester Philharmonic with Howard Hanson in 1931, and then performed by thirty-four other orchestras around the world throughout the 30s. Born in Woodville, Mississippi, and reared in Little Rock, Arkansas, he is popularly known as the "Dean of African-American Composers" and is recognized as one of the great American composers.

Florence Cole-Talbert, a soprano born in 1890, was the first black singer to perform *Aida* with a white European opera company, 1927's Teatro Comunale in Cosenza. She wrote the national hymn of Delta Sigma Theta sorority and was the first black classical artist to record for the historic "race" label, *Black Swan*. She was also the first black director of the Tuskegee Institute's voice department, where she coached **La Julia**

Rhea, a Kentuckian who sang for the National Negro Opera Company and became the first African American to sing with the Chicago Civic Opera Company during the regular season.

Native Mississippian **Ruby Elzy,** one of the greatest soprano voices of her generation, was one of the first inductees into the Mississippi Musicians Hall of Fame. She played the role of Serena in the American folk opera *Porgy and Bess* more than 800 times, and introduced one of the opera's most famous arias, "My Man's Gone Now."

Arturo Toscanini, upon hearing **Marian Anderson's** contralto, said "Yours is a voice one hears once in a hundred years." It is also true that this native Philadelphian's operatic performance on the steps of the Lincoln Memorial on Easter Sunday, April 9, 1939, took on the greatest political significance of any black opera singer in the 20th century. At the time, Anderson had worked her way from opera lessons donated by a local church to a touring career in Europe and on to becoming the country's third highest concert box office draw. When Howard University tried to arrange a concert for her in Constitution Hall, the best indoor location in Washington, D.C., the hall's owners, the Daughters of the American Revolution, refused to allow her to sing there. Protests against the DAR were heard from across the country, including Eleanor Roosevelt, who convinced the Department of Interior to schedule the Easter Concert. More than 75,000 people showed up to the free event, and millions listened on the radio. In 1955, Anderson became the first African American to sing on the stage of New York's Metropolitan Opera House in role of Ulrica in Verdi's *Un Ballo in Maschera*. She received the Presidential Medal of Freedom from President Lyndon Johnson in 1963, and honorary doctorates from over two dozen universities.

The National Symphony, Boston Symphony, the symphony orchestras of Detroit, Minneapolis, Dallas, Buffalo, Denver, London, and the Royal Philharmonic Orchestra have all performed **George Walker's** astounding compositions. He is professor emeritus at Rutgers University. He has over sixty published works and numerous recordings on the various record labels. In 1996, he won the Pulitzer Prize for his composition Lilacs.

Other famous black composers include Samuel Coleridge-Taylor, Anthony Davis, William Dawson, Ulysses Kay, Duke Ellington, Jose Nunes-Garcia, Walter Robinson, Howard Swanson, Edmond Dédé, Henry Thacker Burleigh, Wynton Marsalis, and Florence Beatrice Price.

These are just a few of the hundreds of African American classical musicians and composer that have graced audiences around the world. They are proof that black folks can forge a soulful voice in European art forms, charging them with newfound energy and charm.

Books to check out!

Blacks in Classical Music: A Personal History by Raoul Abdul
An Annotated Catalog of Composers of African Ancestry by Madison H. Carter
My Lord, What a Morning by Marian Anderson

LITERATURE

The Slave Narrative: Tales of Escape

In 1703, a thin autobiography entitled *Adam Negro's Tryall*, by **"Adam, servant of John Saffin, Esq.,"** marked the first time a black slave's story was published, and the beginning of the first black contribution to American literature; the slave narrative. The stories of **Harriet Jacobs, Briton Hammon, George White,** and more than 6,000 others were critical tools in the abolitionist struggle. These authors gave voice to the millions still in bondage by contradicting the claim that black folks were content in bondage to benevolent masters. They also proved, in many cases, that blacks were capable of reading, writing, and reasoning for themselves—negating the charge that people of darker skin were of lower intelligence.

The slave narrative was a genre with specific aims—to rouse shame, disgust and anger regarding slavery among the general population, and to arouse the cry for abolition around the world. The work of this genre also stands as a historical record of the brutality and inhumanity of the "peculiar institution."

While Harriet Beecher Stowe's *Uncle Tom's Cabin* stirred a fire for the cause of abolition in 1852, it should be remembered that it was based on her understanding of the slave narrative. The man upon whom she based her story, **Rev. Josiah Henson,** later wrote his own account of his escape from bondage on the Underground Railroad in *Uncle Tom's Story of His Life.* **Harriet Jacobs**'s *Incidents in the Life of a Slave Girl, Written by Herself* was published in 1861. It provides a moving documentation of her 1834 trek out of slavery in North Carolina, her escape from her master's constant sexual harassment and threats to sell her children.

The most famous slave narrative would easily be **Frederick Douglass**'s *Narrative of the Life of Frederick Douglass, an American Slave, Written by Himself,* first published in 1845. This compelling adventure served as a catalyst for activism throughout the nation. The narrative also details Douglass' thirst for knowledge, his dissatisfaction with a state of illiteracy, and his struggle to teach himself how to read.

After Reconstruction, **Booker T. Washington** also wrote of his childhood as a slave in 1901's *Up From Slavery.* Washington used his oratory skills and autobiography to advocate for learning institutions such as his own Tuskeegee Institute, a college whose mission was to teach basic agricultural and craft skills to newly freed blacks.

In the 1930s, many slave narratives were collected by the Federal Works Progress Administration. These memories can be found in books such as *Bullwhip Days* and *Unchained Memories.* In 2003, **Dr. Henry Louis Gates** published a hand-written book he found in an auction. It turned out to be the first slave narrative novel by a black woman, *The Bondwoman's Narrative*, by **Hannah Crafts.** The book, based on the life of the author, details her story of "passing" for white and making her way to freedom. Slave narratives leave us with a compelling reason and historical precedent to write our own histories down, to pass down the story of our struggles to educate and uplift our community so that others will learn from our example.

Books to check out!

Bullwhip Days: The Slaves Remember: An Oral History Edited with an introduction by James Mellon

Unchained Memories: Readings From the Slave Narratives Foreword by Henry Louis Gates, Jr. with an introduction by Spencer Crew and Cynthia Goodman.

Poets

Yet do I marvel at this curious thing: To make a poet black, and bid him to sing!

—Countee Cullen

Phyllis Wheatley was a Boston slave who could remember being snatched from her native Senegal at a tender age. When she picked up a pen in 1770 and wrote such verse as "On Coming from Africa to America," her master and several prominent townspeople (including John Hancock and Pennsylvania Governor Thomas Hutchinson) had to attest that she had indeed written the poems by herself before they could be marketed in book form. Wheatley's work helped pave the way for poets of the nineteenth century such as **Frances E.W. Harper,** who often used their verse to fortify the abolitionist cause.

At the turn of the twentieth century, Ohio's **Paul Laurence Dunbar** turned to verse. His *Lyrics of a Lowly Life* contained many poems written in dialect, capturing America's imagination. "When Malindy Sings" and "Little Brown Baby" were often recited in black communities throughout the country. One of his contemporaries, **James Weldon Johnson,** wrote a poem to celebrate Abraham Lincoln's birthday, "Lift Every Voice and Sing" in 1900. The song eventually became the Black National Anthem.

Claude McKay was another poet of prowess. His sonnet, "If We Must Die," protested the "Red Summer" race rioting of 1919. In World War II, Winston Churchill used the poem to stir his troops into action.

In the Harlem Renaissance of the 1920s, poets such as **Countee Cullen, Gwendolyn Bennet, Mae Cowdery, Jessie Fausset, Sterling Brown, Robert Hayden,** and **Helene Johnson** began to forge a voice for African Americans through publications such as *Crisis, Fire!!* and *Opportunity* magazines. In 1926, a twenty-four-year-old college dropout wrote a book that shed new light on the possibilities of American literature. **Langston Hughes**'s "The Weary Blues" brought a blues sensibility to American poetry that enriched and influenced writers for generations to come. Hughes is best known for his poetry, but was a master essayist, playwright, and short story writer as well. His literary skill and unaffected air left its mark on an aspiring Chicago poet, **Gwendolyn Brooks,** the first black poet to win the Pulitzer Prize, for *Annie Allen* in 1949. An accomplished poet and novelist, her work helped mentor many black poets from the Black Arts Movement in the 1960s such as **Sonia Sanchez, Haki Madhubuti, Angela Jackson, Sam Greenlee,** and **Sterling Plumpp. Ishmael Reed, Nikki Giovanni,** and **Amiri Baraka** are significant poets that stand out as architects of the Black Arts Movement.

Other black Pulitzer Prize winners include **Rita Dove** in 1987 and **Yusef Komunyakaa** in 1994. American Book Award Winners are **Quincy Troupe, Eugene Redmond, Amiri and Amina Baraka, Etheridge Knight, Ai, Askia Toure, Audre Lorde, Sonia Sanchez, Al Young, Angela Jackson, Ted Joans, Jon Eckels,** and **Lucille Clifton. Ai,** a poet who specializes in personae poems, won the National Book Award in 1999.

Today, new voices in poetry include **Natasha Tretheway, Sharan Strange, Honoree Jeffers, Terrance Hayes, Major Jackson,** and **Kevin Young.** Many of these poets have participated in workshops that nurture black poets into maturity, such as the **Dark Room Collective,** composed of black poets and fiction writers attending northeastern universities in the late 80s and 90s, and the **Cave Canem Workshop,** started by award winning poets **Cornelius Eady** and **Toi Derricotte.** The **Callaloo Workshop,** headed by **Charles Rowell,** is another promising workshop series that has helped foster the next generation of poets. The descendants of slaves are the new griots for the twenty-first century. Their poetry wields the awesome power of truth.

Recommended Poetry Books

Sterling Brown, *Collected Poems*

Wanda Coleman, *Mercurochrome*

Melvin Tolson, *Harlem Gallery*

Michael Harper, *Dear John, Dear Coltrane*

Terrance Hayes, *Hip Logic*

Cornelius Eady, *Brutal Imagination*

Afaa Weaver, *Multitudes*

Lucille Clifton, *The Terrible Stories*

Kevin Young, *Jelly Roll*

Sterling Plumpp, *Velvet BeBop Kente Cloth*

Paul Laurence Dunbar, *Collected Poems*

Amiri Baraka, *Leroi Jones/Amiri Baraka Reader*

Harryette Mullen, *Sleeping With the Dictionary*

Ruth Forman, *We Are the Young Magicians*

Shara McCallum, *The Water Between Us*

Michael Warr, *We Are All the Black Boy*

Lyrae Van Clief Stefanon, *Black Swan*

Thylias Moss, *Rainbow Remnants in Rock Bottom Ghetto Sky*

Willie Perdomo, *Where A Nickel Costs a Dime*

Natasha Trethway, *Domestic Work*

The Last Poets, *On a Mission*

Claude McKay, *Selected Poems*

Carl Phillips, *In the Blood*

Toi Derricotte, *Natural Birth*

Ntozake Shange, *Nappy Edges*

Honi Jeffers, *Gospel of Barbecue*

June Jordan, *Things That I Do in the Dark*

Bob Kaufman, *Cranial Guitar*

Kate Rushin, *The Black Backups*

Patricia Smith, *Life According to Motown*

Ethridge Knight, *The Essential Ethridge Knight*

Yusef Komunyakaa, *Neon Vernacular*

Rita Dove, *Thomas and Beulah*

Sonia Sanchez, *Homegirls and Hand Grenades*

Angela Jackson, *Dark Legs and Silk Kisses*

Maya Angelou, *Poems*

Langston Hughes, *Collected Poems*

Alice Walker, *Revolutionary Petunias*

Kelly Norman Ellis, *Tougaloo Blues*

Tim Seibles, *Hurdy-Gurdy*

G.E. Patterson, *Tug*

A. Van Jordan, *Rise*

Audre Lorde, *Undersong*

Marilyn Nelson, *Fields of Praise*

Essex Hemphill, *Ceremonies*

Regie Gibson, *Storms Beneath the Skin*

Quraysh Ali Lansana, *Southside Rain*

Ai, *Vice*

Elizabeth Alexander, *The Venus Hottentot*

Nikky Finney, *Rice*

Saphire, *American Dreams*

Sharan Strange, *Ash*

Tracie Morris, *Intermission*

Askia Toure, *Dawnsong*

Allison Joseph, *In Every Seam*

Claudia Rankine, *The End of the Alphabet*

Jay Wright, *Transfigurations*

Gwendolyn Brooks, *The Blacks*

Devorah Major, *Sweet Smarts*

Jayne Cortez, *Jazz Fan Looks Back*

Danielle Legros Georges, *Maroon*

Anthologies

The Black Poets, ed. Dudley Randall

Soulfires: Young Black Men on Love and Violence, ed. Wideman, Preston

Role Call: A Generational Anthology, ed. Bashir, Lansana, Medina

Bum Rush the Page: A Def Poetry Jam, ed. Medina, Rivera

Step Into a World: A Global Anthology of Black Literature, ed. Kevin Powell

Making Callaloo: 25 Years of Black Literature, ed. Charles Rowell

Beyond the Frontier: African American Poetry for the 21st Century, ed. Ethelbert Miller

Giant Steps: The New Generation of African American Writers, ed. Keven Young

Cave Canem Anthology Series, ed. Cave Canem

Fiction Writers: Scribes of Our Story

Blacks were forbidden to read or write when brought to this country. Any sign of literacy was punishable by death. This incredible obstacle has made the black contribution to world literature even more remarkable.

Martin Delany, an early advocate of what would be called black nationalism, published *Blake, or the Huts of Africa* as a series of chapters in *The Weekly Anglo-African* during the Civil War. The novel focuses on a West Indian slave who stirs rebellion in the American south and Cuba. **William Wells Brown** penned *Clotel, or The President's Daughter: A Novel of Slave Life*, which was loosely based on **Sarah Hemmings,** the mixed-race daughter of Thomas Jefferson.

After emancipation, the slave narrative was put aside for literature that more adequately addressed current issues. Blacks had the opportunity to explore the many nuances of newfound freedom through fiction. It did not take long before marvelous works of literature blossomed in the American landscape. **Sutton Griggs** explored the possibilities of a freed black state in Texas with *Imperium in Imperio*. **Frances E.W. Harper** wrote *Iola Leroy* and *Moses: A Story of the Nile*, both of which were quite popular in the nineteenth century. Her short story "The Two Offers" is said to be the first of that genre by a black woman in the U.S.

In the early 1900's, **Charles William Chesnutt** created such masterpieces as *The Marrow of Tradition* and *The Conjure Woman Tales*, works that explored the jagged edge of the color line in black society and the ante-bellum south. In 1923, **Jean Toomer** published *Cane*, a poetic novel about the changing southland that is still innovative a century later. It is impossible to measure the impact of such novels as **Richard Wright**'s *Black Boy*, **Ann Petry**'s *The Street*, or **Zora Neale Hurston**'s *Their Eyes Were Watching God*. **Nella Larsen** wrote *Quicksand*, a semiautobiographical novel about a mixed race woman in search of identity—the novel won the Harmon Foundation Prize.

In 1952, **Ralph Ellison** published what has been regarded as one of the most important novels of the century, *Invisible Man*. This surreal trip through the life of a nameless black protagonist left readers amazed by its complexity and daring. It won the 1953 National Book Award. Other National Book Award winners include **Alice Walker** and **Charles Johnson.**

Black Pulitzer prizewinners include **James Alan McPherson** in 1980 for *Elbow Room* and **Toni Morrison** for *Beloved* in 1988. Morrison joined poet/playwrights **Derek Walcott** and **Wole Soyinka** as black Nobel Prize winners in 1993. American Book Award Winners include

Tananarive Due, Edwidge Danticat, Trey Ellis, Toni Cade Bambara, Paule Marshall, Terry McMillan, Toni Morrison, and **John Edgar Wideman.** Black science fiction writers **Samuel Delaney** and **Octavia Butler** have both won Nebula Awards. **Walter Mosley** and **Valerie Wilson Wesley** are prominent mystery writers with a growing audience.

Toni Bambara, Henry Dumas, Ernest Gaines, Chester Himes, Gayl Jones, James O. Killens, Clarence Major, Gloria Naylor, and **Claude Brown** have impacted readers around the world with their stories. This legacy will only grow as more black writers come of age. Today, new writers such as **Colson Whitehead, ZZ Packard, Danzy Senna,** and **Percival Everett** are creating new vistas of imagination.

Below is a short list of fascinating fiction from African American authors:

Chinua Achebe, *Things Fall Apart*

Nella Larsen, *Quicksand*

Maya Angelou, *I Know Why the Caged Bird Sings*

Victor D. Lavalle, *Slapboxing With Jesus*

James Baldwin, *Giovanni's Room*

Terry Macmillan, *Disappearing Acts*

Gwendolyn Brooks, *Maud Martha*

Toni Morrison, *Beloved*

Bebe Moore Campbell, *Brothers and Sisters*

Paule Marshall, *Brown Girl/ Brownstones*

Cyrus Colter, *The Beach Umbrella*

Walter Moseley, *Always Outnumbered, Always Outgunned*

Tananarive Due, *My Soul to Keep*

Gloria Naylor, *Women of Brewster Place*

Henry Dumas, *Echo Tree*

Z.Z. Packer, *Drinking Coffee Elsewhere*

Percival Everett, *Erasure*

Ann Petry, *The Street*

Jessie Fausett, *Plum Bun*

Ishmael Reed, *Mumbo Jumbo*

Arthur Flowers, *Another Good Lovin' Blues*

Jewell Parker Rhodes, *Voodoo Dreams*

Ernest Gaines, *A Lesson Before Dying*

Ntozake Shange, *Sassafrass, Cypress & Indigo*

Marita Goldin, *Long Distance Life*

Sheree R. Thomas, *Dark Matter*

E. Lynn Harris, *Just As I Am*

Jean Toomer, *Cane*

Chester Himes, *If He Hollers, Let Him Go*

Alice Walker, *The 3rd Life of Grange Copeland*

James Weldon Johnson, *Autobiography of an Ex-Colored Man*

John Edgar Wideman, *Fever*

Randall Kenan, *Let the Dead Bury Their Dead*

Colson Whitehead, *The Intutionist*

Jamaica Kincaid, *Autobiography of My Mother*

Shay Youngblood, *The Big Mama Stories*

Playwrights and Theatre Companies: Griots of the Stage

Black playwrights and theatre companies defined themselves by their efforts to depict black humanity and depth outside the stereotypical restrictions of minstrelsy. As early as 1821, a black acting troupe known as the **African Company** presented Shakespearean plays to the populace of New York. Headed by Caribbean actor **James Hewlett,** the company founded the **African Theatre,** a theater for black patrons who were tired of sitting in segregated seats of white theaters. In the late nineteenth century, **Bob Cole** started a black stock theatre company in Greenwich Village, and produced the first black operetta, *The Shoofly Regiment.* In 1858, **William Wells Brown** became the first published black playwright with his play *The Escape, or A Leap for Freedom.*

Bert Williams and **George Walker** formed the team of Williams and Walker, and with writer/director/actor **Jesse Shipp** they tried to break out of minstrelsy and blackface. 1908's *Bandanna Land* satirized white people's fear of integration. Meanwhile, at the **Crescent Theater** in Harlem, **Eddie Hunter** wrote and appeared in plays such as 1909's

Subway Sal. The Crescent also featured *The Tryst*, penned by **Harry Freeman.**

In 1916, **Angelina Weld Grimke**'s play *Rachel* depicted the horrors of lynching, and the following year, **Ridgely Torrence** produced *Three Plays for a Negro Theatre.* In 1921, *Shuffle Along* exploded onto the stage. Written by **Flournoy Miller, Aubrey Lyles, Noble Sissle,** and **Eubie Blake,** this all-black musical comedy starred **Florence Mills** and **Josephine Baker**. Later, in 1925, **Zora Neale Hurston**'s *Color Struck* won an Opportunity award. The play reflected on Zora's Florida childhood and color discrimination within the black community. In the '30s **Rose McClendon** and **Dick Campbell** founded the **Negro People's Theatre,** and they produced a black version of Clifford Odetes' *Waiting for Lefty.* **Shirley Graham Dubois** became the first black woman to produce an all-black opera, *Tom Tom.* **Langston Hughes**'s *Mulatto* appeared in 1934, and was later adopted into an opera, *The Barrier.* Hughes went on to found the **Harlem Suitcase Theatre** with **Hilary Phillips** in 1938, launching experimental plays such as *Don't You Want to Be Free?* in a Harlem loft.

In 1940, writer Abram Hill and actor Frederick O'Neal founded the **American Negro Theatre** (ANT). Over 50,000 people would see young stars such as **Sidney Poitier** and **Ruby Dee** in ANT shows over the next decade. ANT helped launch the career of **Alice Childress,** the first African American to win an Obie Award for 1955's *Trouble in Mind.* 1955 also saw the successful Broadway run of **James Baldwin**'s *Amen Corner.*

Baldwin's work served as a bridge toward the Black Arts Movement's flurry of new plays that were eager to break new ground. **Amiri Baraka**'s *The Dutchman* startled audiences out of complacency with its searing indictment of American cultural values. In 1965, **Lorraine Hansberry** became the first black woman to write and direct a Broadway play—and the youngest to win a New York Drama Critic's Circle Award. *Raisin in the Sun*, based on a black Chicago family's struggle to find suitable housing despite discrimination, is still widely anthologized today.

By 1971, New York's **Black Theatre Alliance** emerged, dedicated to the production of black plays. In Chicago, **Abena Joan Brown** founded **ETA Creative Arts Foundation** for the same purpose. **Ed Bullins,** former Black Panther Party Minister of Culture, had managed theatre production in Oakland, California's **Black House** until he moved to New York and won the 1971 Obie Award for *The Fabulous Miss Marie*. At the same time, **Ntozake Shange** was perfecting a new concept: a poem that could be performed by several actors. The result, *For Colored Girls Who Have Considered Suicide/When the Rainbow is Enuf: A Choreopoem*, won the 1977 Obie Awards, and is still performed in many theatres today.

In 1984, **August Wilson**'s play *Ma Rainey's Black Bottom* was produced on Broadway and won Best Play of the Year by the New York Drama Critics' Circle. His plays *Fences* and *The Piano Lesson* both won Pulitzer Prizes.

Ana Deveare Smith's *Fires in the Mirror and Twilight* and **George C. Wolfe**'s *Colored Museum* are major award-winning contributions to the

American stage. **Reg E. Gaines**'s *Bring in Da Noise, Bring in Da Funk* won huge critical acclaim on Broadway, and **Suzan Lori-Parks**'s *Topdog/Underdog* won a 2003 Pulitzer Prize. Black playwrights and theatre companies have come a long way from minstrelsy in their effort to portray a fully humanistic view of their people.

Herstory: Black Women's Fiction and Poetry

Because the many obstacles of sexism and racism in the United States have traditionally stifled black women's voices, it has been a tremendous struggle for black women writers to be heard. In the past, women wrote in relative obscurity. The first black woman author was **Phyllis Wheatley,** who published her poetry in 1770. In her wake, black women have had a tremendous record of writing their stories and contributing to the patchwork of American literature.

In the nineteenth century, many black women penned autobiographies and slave narratives. **Octavia Albert** collected slave narratives that would later become the book *House of Bondage*. Other women authors of the time include **Ann Plato, Mary Prince, Adah Mencken,** and **Hallie Brown,** who penned *Bits and Odds* and *Homespun Heroines*.

In the twentieth century, many more sisters of color started to come to the fore of publishing. **Nella Larsen** produced *Passing* and *Quicksand*. Columbia-trained anthropologist **Zora Neale Hurston**'s *Their Eyes Were Watching God* is still a poetic *tour de force* today. In 1945, **Ann**

Petry's *The Street* broke new ground with a major publisher, Houghton Mifflin. In 1950, **Gwendolyn Brooks** became the first African American to win the Pulitzer Prize in poetry for her book, *Annie Allen*.

Paule Marshall and **Audre Lorde,** both of Caribbean descent and born in New York, added their voices to the canon of American literature. Marshall's *Browngirl, Brownstone* recreated her Brooklyn childhood, and *Soul Clap Hands and Sing* won her the National Institute of Arts Award. Audre Lorde's self-identification as a lesbian of color sang throughout her poetry in *Cables to Rage, Black Unicorn*, and *The Cancer Journals*.

In the 1960s, **Gayle Jones**'s *Corregidora* and *Eva's Man* set new standards in American fiction. In the 70s and beyond, Alice Walker helped evolve a new definition of women-based theory and activism: womanist (or womynist) thought. Walker defined the term as "Wanting to know more and in greater depth than is considered 'good' for one. Interested in grown up doings. Acting grown up. Being grown up. Interchangeable with another black folk expression: 'You trying to be grown.' Responsible. In charge. Serious. . . . Womanist is to feminist what lavender is to purple." Walker also helped break silence about issues of abuse with her books *The Color Purple* and *Possessing the Secret of Joy*. **Toni Morrison** won the Pulitzer Prize for her *Beloved,* while **Terry McMillan** had a runaway hit with *Waiting to Exhale,* and is the best selling black author of all time. Other women who have created new spaces for themselves between the pages of America's literary canon include **Gloria Naylor,** whose *Women of Brewster Place* and *Linden Hills* are fiction masterpieces. A native Antiguan who has made the U.S. her home, **Jamaica Kincaid** has captured readers' imaginations with *Autobiography of My Mother* and *Lucy*.

In poetry, three women have won the prestigious Cave Canem award for a first book in poetry, **Natasha Tretheway, Tracy K. Smith,** and **Lyrae Van Clief-Stefanon.** Other prestigious upcoming women poets include **Honoree Jeffers, Angela Shannon,** and **Tracie Morris.**

Black women have created a new space for themselves in the canon of American and World Literature. It is impossible to completely understand the history and struggle of black folks in America without understanding the story of black women. These women of color have made their voices loud and clear through their fantastic fiction and compelling poetry.

ARTISTS AND ARTISANS

Molding Stories from Stone: Black Sculptors and Three-Dimensional Artists

Throughout America's history, black people have molded clay, wood, concrete, and steel to make images that reflect their unique journey. **Eugene Warburg** of New Orleans was an accomplished black sculptor whose work, except for a bust of John Young Mason, is mostly lost. He died in Europe in 1867. In that same year, **Edmonia Lewis** moved to Rome to enjoy the more racially tolerant atmosphere, and to sculpt masterpieces from Italy's excellent marble. Born in 1840 to a black father and Chippewa mother, Lewis was the first internationally acclaimed black sculptor. A graduate of Oberlin College, her marble statue *The Dying Cleopatra* won an award at the American Centennial Exposition of 1876. While she spent much of her career in Rome, Lewis' neoclassical style powerfully addressed the histories of Native and African American people in work such as *Forever Free* and *The Marriage of Hiawatha*. Lewis won commissions of up to $50,000 and was quite successful before she died in the 1890s, not long before **Meta Vaux Warrick** ventured to the Colarossi Academy in Paris to study sculpture in 1899.

Warrick, who received praise from Rodin, exhibited at the Paris Salon in 1903. She returned to the U.S. to produce work such as *Water Boy*, but much of her work was lost in a 1910 fire.

By 1928, a Boston born orphan by the name of **Sargent Claude Johnson** entered and won a competition for the Otto H. Kahn Prize with his ceramic bust *Sammy*. Johnson aimed to produce "a strictly Negro art" that would speak directly to his people. His public art produced through the Works Progress Administration (WPA), such as an athletic relief sculpture mural at San Francisco's George Washington High School, are still in place today.

Augusta Savage was born to a poor Florida family, but was one of the first women to study sculpture at New York's Cooper Union. She was about to drop out of school for lack of funds when she received a commission to do a bust of W.E.B. DuBois. Her work was so exemplary that in 1930 she won a Rosenwald grant for her bust of a Harlem youth, *Gamin*. Savage eventually became a project supervisor for the WPA, producing work such as *Lift Every Voice and Sing*. Her contemporary in Chicago was **Richmond Barthe,** who featured work in the Whitney Museum and the Metropolitan Museum of Art. Other sculptors such as **Selma Burke** and **William E. Artis** achieved recognition through their intriguing and life-like imagery in stone.

Elizabeth Catlett is accomplished in painting, linocuts and sculpture. Catlett's pursuit of technique took her to Mexico's Taller de Grafica Popular, where collective study taught her to base her work on people's needs. *Black Unity*, the fist she carved out of wood in 1968, expressed the call for independence.

Other black sculptors include **Betye and Alison Saar,** a mother and daughter whose art combines wood, metal, glass, painting, and found objects. Today, contemporary artists like **George Smith, Osmond Watson, Charnelle Holloway, Barbara Chase Rimbaud,** and **Stephanie Johnson** use metal, paper, bronze, gold, and silk to construct vivid, living sculpture that breathes of the past and exhales the future. These artists, and those who follow in their tradition, chisel, weld, carve, hammer, and paint a new vision for black people.

Books to check out!

Emancipation and the Freed in American Sculpture by Freeman H. Murray

In Our Own Image: Black Painters

African American painters have left a stunning legacy on canvass. From **Edward Bannister** and **Elizabeth Catlett** to **Jean Michel Basquiat** and **Kara Walker,** black hands wielding paintbrushes have left their indelible mark on the American psyche.

One of the earliest known black painters was **Joshua Johnston,** a former slave who practiced his art from the 1790s to at least 1826. This Baltimorean portrait artist's fame was widespread among the merchants of Maryland and Virginia. **Sarah Mapps Douglass,** born in 1806, was also a painter and abolitionist of the time.

Robert S. Duncanson was born in 1821 in New York State and grew up near Cincinnati. After studying in Italy and returning to America, he was praised by the Cincinnati Gazette as "the best landscape painter in the West." Johnston and Duncanson's successes helped erode the myth of black inferiority. Nevertheless, that myth persisted. In 1876, a *New York Herald* commentary stated, "the Negro seems to have an appreciation of art, while being manifestly unable to produce it." When **Edward**

M. Bannister, an aspiring black Bostonian painter, read that comment he became manifestly determined to disprove it. His painting *Under the Oaks* won a bronze medal at the 1876 Centennial Exposition in Philadelphia.

Henry O. Tanner may be the most famous black artist of the 19th century. Born in Pittsburgh and schooled in Europe, his paintings such as *The Banjo Lesson* reflect a mastery of light and setting. He later participated in the Paris Salon of 1894, and by 1906 his *Two Disciples at the Tomb* won the Harris Prize at the Art Institute of Chicago, and was elected a member of the National Academy of Design in 1909. He died in Paris in 1937, but not without having mentored black artists such as **Aaron Douglass** and **William A. Harper.**

The 1920s proved to be a time when the floodgates of black creativity were thrown wide open, and painting was no exception. **Aaron Douglass**'s work was featured in one of the defining anthologies of the Harlem Renaissance, *The New Negro,* and he is best known for the series he created for James Weldon Johnson's *God's Trombones.* His work, along with that of **Palmer Hayden** and **Archibald Motley** attempted to recall a romanticized vision of Africa. In 1929, Motley became the first artist of any race to receive front-page coverage in the *New York Times.*

Other prominent artists such as **William H. Johnson, Horace Pippin,** and **Jacob Lawrence** were known as neo-primitivists for their ability to capture the dynamism and raw energy of the black aesthetic. Lawrence, born in 1917, learned in Harlem art classes from **Charles Alston,** who had created cover illustrations for the *New Yorker.*

Lawrence's narrative paintings on the life of Harriet Tubman, Frederick Douglass, and Toussaint L'Ouverture helped inspire the *John Brown* series of **Horace Pippin.** Pippin, who was a corporal in the 369th during WWI, had received a serious shoulder injury during combat. Nevertheless, he was determined to paint masterpieces, and joined the ranks of black artists such as **Lois Mailou Jones,** a Bostonian whose expressionist and impressionist work won the Robert Woods Bliss Award in 1941.

Romare Bearden, a cartoonist turned painter who later became renowned for his use of collage, started painting seriously after World War 2 and created a plethora of memorable pieces such as *Gardens of Babylon* and *Return of the Prodigal Son.* His sense of activism for black artists is matched by **Margaret Burroughs,** a painter and woodcut artist who later established the first African American history and culture museum in the U.S., the DuSable Museum.

Other great black artists include **Elizabeth Catlett,** whose paintings, sculptures, and lithographs confirmed her position as a master American artist. Painters such as **Dox Thrash, Walter Williams, Yvonne Catchings, Robin Holder, Vivian Browne,** and **Calvin Burnett** provided stunning canvasses to galleries across the world throughout the 60s and 70s. In the 80s, **Jean Michel Basquiat** stepped to the fore, and was the youngest artist ever to showcase at the Whitney Museum when he was twenty-two. **Philemona Williamson** also started exhibiting in the 80s, and was later awarded a grant from the National Endowment for the Arts.

Today, Macarthur Genius Grant recipient **Kara Walker**'s intriguing and provocative silhouettes provide a new frontier of visual expression along with the work of artists such as **Gilda Snowden, Deborah Muirhead, Kerry James Marshall, Michael Ray Charles,** and **Marcus Akinlana.**

Black artists continue to raise interesting questions in new and exciting ways in their work, wrapping their multi-hued canvasses around new generations.

Books to check out!

African American Art and Artists by Samella Lewis
African-American Art by Sharon F. Patton

Through a Sepia Lens: Black Photographers

The earliest form of photography, the daguerreotype, was born in France in 1839. The first black person to have a public showing of his work was **Jules Lion.** Lion, a black expatriate of France, had exhibited award-winning lithographs at the 1833 Exposition of Paris. In 1840, he was the first daguerreotypist of any color in New Orleans to exhibit work at the St. Charles Museum. By 1875, there were at least fifty black daguerreotypists with successful galleries across the country, including **James Presley Ball** and **Augustus Washington.** Both artists used their skills to highlight the savagery of slavery. Ball, a free Virginian born in 1825, was an itinerant daguerreotypist who eventually settled in Cincinnati and opened the **Great Daguerrean Gallery of the West.** His exhibits, such as *Ball's Splendid Mammoth Pictorial Tour of the United States Comprising Views of the African Slave Trade*, gave witness and voice to the cause for abolition. Ball continued his vocation in several cities until his 1904 death in Hawaii. Trenton native Augustus Washington, son of an ex-slave and an Asian mother, opened a studio in Hartford in the

1840s. He took a famous portrait of John Brown standing next to the American flag, but grew steadily discouraged by American racism and eventually migrated to Liberia in 1853, where he continued to take portraits of émigrés. **Glenalvin** and **Wallace Goodridge, Harry Shepherd,** and **George O. Brown** all operated successful studios as the art of photography advanced in the late nineteenth century. **Daniel Freeman** opened a studio in Washington, D.C., and started the Washington Amateur Art Society.

In the beginning of the twentieth century, scores of black photographers served a population that often did not have access to services in white communities. Three of the most influential of the time were **Arthur Bedou, Cornelius Battey,** and **James VanDerZee.** Battey, born in Augusta, Georgia, established a reputation with his successful studios in Cleveland and New York, and directed the Photography Division of Tuskeegee Institute in 1916. His portraits of famous black leaders are legendary even today, and his work won international awards while appearing on the covers of *Opportunity* and *Crisis* magazines.

Arthur Bedou, a New Orleans native, won awards for his work, and was published in many periodicals. James VanDerZee is the best-known black photographer of the era before WWII. Harlem was his studio, and the faces of his people were a constant subject for this Massachusetts native whose parents were servants to President Ulysses S. Grant. His work got national recognition at New York's Museum of Modern Art in 1968, and he received the President's Living Legacy Award in 1978.

In Washington, D.C., **Robert H. McNeil** recorded the lives of black women domestic workers and their arduous search for work in a series called *The Bronx Slave Market*, which appeared in the black owned magazine *Flash!* Another contributor to *Flash!* was **"Teenie" Harris,** a self taught Pittsburgh photographer who documented the regular and celebrity lives of black folks in the famous steel town.

Other photographers of the time include **King Daniel Ganaway, James Latimer Allen, Addison N. Scurlock, Richard Twine,** and **Andrew Kelly.** A prominent black woman photographer of the time was **Elnora Teal,** who ran a successful studio in Houston, Texas with her husband from 1919 to 1948. **Eslanda Robeson** also used photography as an anthropological tool throughout her worldwide travels.

In 1937, young photographer **Gordon Parks** trained with the Farm Security Administration, and completed some portraits of Ella Watson, a black domestic worker. The series, *American Gothic, Washington, D.C., 1942,* won him wide acclaim. Parks became the first African American to work on the staff of *Life* Magazine, and went on to become a successful novelist, filmmaker, and composer. Still other great photographers of the time include **Roy DeCarava, Richard Saunders, Chuck Stewart** (who photographed many famous jazz musicians), **Bob Moore,** and **Ernest C. Withers.**

Today, black photographers continue to capture America in an aperture of their own creation. **Jeanne Moutoussamy-Ashe, Joe Harris, Don Camp, Dawoud Bey, Lynn Marshall Linnemeir, Clarissa Sligh, Pat Ward Williams, Albert Chong, Accra Shepp, Camille Gustus, Shelia Turner, Linda L. Ammons, David C. Driskell, Anthony Beale,** and

Wendel White are all accomplished contemporary photographers who have won awards and are regularly featured in exhibits. Anthologies of black photography such as Deborah Willis' *Reflections In Black*, Jeanne Moutoussamy-Ashe's *Viewfinders: Black Women Photographers*, and Charles Roland's *Life in a Day of Black L.A* give us a glimpse of ourselves that was created with our own fingers on the button.

Books to check out!

Reflections in Black: A History of Black Photographers, 1840 to the Present Day by Deborah Willis-Thomas
Viewfinders: Black Women Photographers by Jeanne Moutoussamy-Ashe

Some Famous Actors

There are quite a few famous black actors. Here we will pause to give notice to a few: **Sidney Poitier** won 1964's best actor Oscar for his role in *Lilies of the Field*. **Hattie McDaniel** won an Oscar for her role in 1939's *Gone with the Wind*. These were the only black actors to win America's highest award for acting until 2002, when **Denzel Washington** won for *Training Day* and **Halle Berry** won honors for *Monster's Ball*.

Some memorable performances of black actors include **Ivan Dixon, Abbey Lincoln,** and **Stanley Greene** in *Nothing But a Man*. **Dorothy Dandridge** had riveting roles in *Carmen Jones* and *Porgy and Bess*. **Paul Robeson** gave a memorable performance in *Emperor Jones*, and played a stunning lead role in *Othello*. **Laurence Fishburn** and **Angela Basset** were explosive in *What's Love Got to Do With It,* the story of Ike and Tina Turner. **Sidney Poitier, Claudia McNeil, Ruby Dee, Diana Sands, Ivan Dixon, Louis Gossett Jr.,** and **Stephen Perry** did a magnificent job in the film version of Lorraine Hansberry's *Raisin in the*

Sun. **Ethel Waters**'s role in *Member of the Wedding* is the first time a black actress carried a white major studio production. **Harry Belafonte** played incredible roles in *Carmen Jones, Island in the Sun,* and *Uptown Saturday Night,* which costarred **Bill Cosby, Sidney Poitier, Flip Wilson** and **Richard Pryor. Andre Braugher, Mario Van Peebles,** and **Charles Dutton** have starred in quite a few movie and TV roles, including *10,000 Black Men Named George.*

These are just some of the famous black actors and actresses that have graced the silver screen and TV.

Vin Diesel (*XXX*), Ving Rhames (*Mission Impossible*), Gregory Hines (*Tap*), Don Cheadle (*Lesson Before Dying*), Viveca Fox (*Kill Bill*), Redd Fox (*Harlem Nights*), Morgan Freeman (*Bruce Almighty*), Pam Grier (*Foxy Brown*), Eartha Kitt (*Holes*), Bernie Mac (*Charlies Angels: Full Throttle*), Roger Mosley (*Leadbelly*), Joe Morton (*Ali*), Nichelle Nichols (*Star Trek*), Ron O'Neal (*Superfly*), Mekhi Phifer (*O*), Della Reese (*Having Our Say: The Delaney Sister's First 100 Years*), Esther Rolle (*Rosewood*), John Amos (*The Players Club*), Tupac Shakur (*Juice*), Robert Townsend (*The Five Heartbeats*), Spike Lee (*Do The Right Thing*), Leslie Uggams (*Roots*), Gabrielle Union (*Bad Boys 2*), Blair Underwood (*Full Frontal*), Vanessa Williams (*Light It Up*), Forest Whitaker (*Ghost Dog*), Billy Dee Williams (*Mahogany*), Oprah Winfrey (*The Color Purple*), Alfre Woodard (*Down in the Delta*), N'Bushe Wright (*Blade*), Paul Winfield, Chris Tucker (*Rush Hour 3*), Cicely Tyson (*The Autobiography of Miss Jane Pittman*), Wesley Snipes (*Blade*), Will Smith

(*Ali*), Richard Pryor (*Jo Jo Dancer, Your Life Is Calling*), Jada Pinkett Smith (*Matrix Revolutions*), Chris Rock (*Head of State*), Mos Def (*Monster*), Thandie Newton (*The Truth About Charlie*), Butterfly McQueen (*Seven Wishes of a Rich Kid*), Nia Long (*The Best Man*), DelRoy Lindo (*Malcom X*), LL Cool J (*Rollerball*), Ice Cube (*Barbershop*), Beyonce Knowles (*Austin Powers in Goldmember*), Orlando Jones (*Biker Boyz*), Lauryn Hill (*Restaurant*), Robin Harris (*Do the Right Thing*), Danny Glover (*Beloved*), Ossie Davis (*Jungle Fever*), Lisa Bonet (*Lathe of Heaven*), Oprah Winfrey (*Beloved*).

VOCATIONS

Blacks in the Military: Buffalo Soldiers

Blacks have a long and admirable history of military service for America. This tradition of valor goes back to the Revolutionary War, when **Crispus Attucks** was the first to fall in the Boston Massacre, and Captain John Paul Jones praised his two black seamen, **Cato** and **Scipio,** as "prime seamen."

A Maryland black militiaman, **Nicholas Biddle,** was the first to lose his life fighting Confederates in 1861. In March of 1863, the Enrollment Act allowed for conscription of all male citizens into the Union Army— including blacks. Black volunteers came from all over the United States and parts of Canada in order to fight against slavery. Young and old, freemen and former slaves, illiterate and learned, all of them wanted an opportunity to fight for freedom. Over 178,000 black troops fought heroically at Fort Wagner, Olustee, Milliken's Bend, and Port Hudson, with over 36,000 casualties. **Frederick Douglass** summed up their thoughts when he said, "Once let the black man get upon his person the brass letters 'U.S.,' let him get an eagle on his button and a musket on his shoulder and bullets in his pockets and there is no power on earth which can deny that he has earned the right to citizenship in the United States."

After the Civil War, the **Ninth and Tenth Cavalry,** and the **24th** and **25th Infantry Regiments** were organized for the Indian Wars. They were known as **Buffalo Soldiers** to their combatants, and were instrumental in the country's expansion west. All four regiments later served in Cuba during the Spanish American War, where they were instrumental in the Battle of San Juan Hill and five of them earned a Medal of Honor. Buffalo Soldiers also served in the Philippines from 1899 to 1902.

During World War I, blacks served in the **93rd Provisional Division,** which was among the first American forces to arrive in France. Black troops were also included in the **369th, 370th, 371st,** and **372nd** divisions. Nearly 400,000 black doughboys served in Europe, and 171 of them were awarded the Croix de Guerre.

Benjamin O. Davis survived four years of the silent treatment at West Point Academy to become the nation's first black general during World War II. In 1942, he became the first black officer to pilot an Army Air Corps aircraft solo while training with the **Tuskeegee Airmen,** one of the most successful fighter groups in the U.S. Army Air Corps. These black pilots flew over 15,000 sorties in Europe during the final years of the war, destroying 251 aircraft and winning more than 850 medals. They never lost a single bomber that they escorted on a bombing run into Europe. One of their crew was **Daniel "Chappie" James Jr.,** who later became the Air Force's first black four-star general in 1975, the same year that the Army's appointed its first black four-star general, **Roscoe Robinson Jr.** These advances were possible because of their sterling service and the fact that in 1948 President Harry Truman signed Executive Order No. 9981, eliminating discrimination in the military. This opened up new horizons for black soldiers like **Carl Brashear,** who became the Navy's first black Master Diver in 1963.

Black soldiers served with distinction in Korea, particularly in the all-black **2nd, 3rd,** and **25th Army Infantry Divisions** and the **159th Field Artillery Battalion** and the **77th Engineer Combat Company.** The 159th never lost a gun to the enemy, and two soldiers, **Private 1st Class William Thompson** and **Sgt. Cornelius H. Charlton,** were posthumously awarded the first Medals of Honor to black fighting men since the Spanish-American War. In Vietnam, black soldiers served with distinction, receiving more than their portion of casualties in combat. **Colin Powell,** a former Vietnam vet, led soldiers in Panama and Vietnam, and conducted diplomacy during both Gulf Wars. He was named Secretary of State in 2000. There are now over 150 active or retired black generals.

Today, the armed forces may be the most integrated employment sector in the U.S., thanks to those who sacrificed in the past.

Books to check out!

African American Military Heroes by Jim Haskins

African American Generals and Flag Officers: Biographies of over 120 Blacks in the United States Military by Walter L. Hawkins

The Right to Fight: A History of African Americans in the Military by Gerald Astor

The Tuskegee Airmen
"Red-Tailed Black Angels"

On June 25, 1944, over the Adriatic Sea's Trieste Harbor, a squadron of American P-51 Mustangs flew into a morning sky thick with flak. Their planes' red tails sliced through the air toward a German destroyer that had every gun on deck firing away at the men sitting in the plane's cockpits. **Captain John Elsberry** swooped in for the first attack, his fifty caliber machine guns blazing bullets at the battleship's crew. Following him was **Lt. Henry Scott, Airmen Joe Lewis, Charles Dunne, Wendell Pruitt,** and **Gwynne Pierson,** each facing flak and bullets head on, their machine guns ripping into the battleship. On Pruitt's pass, his accurate fire set the ship ablaze, and Pierson's pass, a direct hit on ammunition or fuel, sparked an explosion that nearly rocked his plane out of the sky. Minutes later the destroyer sunk, marking the first and only time that a warship was destroyed solely by airplane machine gun fire during World War II. The pilots that pulled off this incredible feat were flying not only for their country, but for their pride and the honor of their people—they were African American pilots of the 332nd Fighter group.

Such were the exploits of the Tuskegee Airmen, the **332nd Fighter Group** of the U.S. Army Air Force, a combination of the 100th, 301st, and 302nd Tuskegee squadrons.

On July 19, 1941, the AAF began an experimental program at Booker T. Washington's famous **Tuskegee Institute** in Alabama to train blacks as military pilots. Young men from Detroit, Chicago, Portsmouth, Cleveland, Pasadena, Tarboro, and all points in between filled out applications to Aviation Cadet Training and flocked to Tuskegee to pass the rigorous tests and make the grade to fly against the enemy. The first classes were trained to be fighter pilots for the famous 99th Fighter Squadron, slated for combat duty in North Africa. The "Tuskegee Experiment" eventually graduated over 900 pilots, 450 of whom were sent overseas for combat assignment, with 66 destined to lose their lives on combat flights. Some of the famous Tuskegee Division of Aeronautics graduates include Four-Star General **Daniel "Chappie" James,** who went on to fly over 160 combat missions in Korea and Vietnam, and **Benjamin O. Davis Jr.,** the son of General Davis Sr., who went on to become a Four-Star General himself. **Captain Lee A. Archer** was the Tuskegee Airmen's ace, with at least five confirmed aerial kills in 169 combat missions over more than 11 countries.

The Tuskegee Airmen, or **"Red Tails,"** as they were known for the color painted on their tail wings, flew more than 15,000 sorties, destroyed over 1,000 German aircraft, and received more then 150 Distinguished Flying Crosses while flying 1,578 missions with the 12th Tactical U.S. Army Air Force and the 15th Strategic U.S. Army Air Force.

They also earned 744 Air Medals, 8 Purple Hearts, and 14 Bronze Stars during their deployment in combat. Flying a wide range of aircraft, such as Curtiss P-40L War Hawks, Bell P-39 Airacobras, Republic P-47 Thunderbolts, and P-51 Mustangs, these black aviators shredded stereotypes about black inferiority when they consistently carried out battle plans and gained the trust of skeptical white pilots by saving their lives time after time. While assigned to escort bombers, they achieved their greatest claim to fame: *they were the only U.S. Fighter Group in World War II that could claim to have never lost a bomber in their care.* They earned the nickname "Red-Tailed Black Angels" because of their amazing record.

At times, Tuskegee fliers had to protest segregationist policies of the military. In April of 1945, 101 black officers of the 477th, a black bomber-training group led by **2nd Lt. Roger C. Terry** and **Lt. Marsden Thompson,** entered a segregated officers Club at Freeman Field, Indiana and refused to leave until arrested. They later refused a direct order from their commanding officer to endorse a regulation that supported the segregation and were court-martialed. Their protest put pressure on the War Department and helped lead to President Harry Truman's **Executive Order 9981.** The order, passed in 1948, ended racial segregation within the ranks of the United States military forces. Fifty years later, Terry had become president of Tuskegee Airmen, Inc., and was exonerated of the court-martial charges.

On November 6, 1998, President Clinton approved Public Law 105-355, establishing the **Tuskegee Airmen National Historic Site** at Moton

Field in Tuskegee, Alabama. The site commemorates the heroic actions of the Tuskegee Airmen during World War II.

It is important to remember that these black men fought for race pride as well as patriotism. They fought a war on two fronts: the war for respect at home and the war for victory against the Axis powers. They were eventually successful on both fronts.

Books to check out!

Lonely Eagles: the Story of America's Black Air Force in World War II by Robert A. Rose

The Tuskegee Airmen: The Men Who Changed a Nation by Charles E. Francis

Segregated Skies: All-Black Combat Squadrons of WW II by Stanley Sandler

The Tuskegee Airmen Mutiny at Freeman Field by Lt. Col. James C. Warren

Black Astronauts: Claiming the Stars

On December 8, 1997, thirty years after his death, **Major Robert Lawrence Jr.**'s name was engraved into the Astronauts Memorial Foundation's Space Mirror Memorial. Lawrence, the first black astronaut, died in a jet crash in 1967. Although Lawrence was a member of the Air Force's Manned Orbital Laboratory, and was the Air Force's first "negro astronaut designee," it took thirty years of constant pressure from his family and friends to get acknowledgement for his contribution to his country.

Eleven years after his death, the next black trainees gained admission to NASA's program in 1978. In 1983, the first of them to venture into outer space was former Tuskeegee Airman and Vietnam Veteran, **Guion Bluford,** who served as a mission specialist aboard the space shuttle *Challenger*. Bluford was an aerospace engineer with a Ph.D. from the Air Force Institute of Technology.

Ron McNair was the next black astronaut to strap on a helmet. McNair was a fifth degree karate black belt, and an accomplished saxophone player with a Ph.D. in physics from Massachusetts Institute of

Technology. He had logged 191 hours in space before the fatal crash of the *Challenger*, which exploded 73 seconds after launch on January 26, 1986.

Frederick Gregory was the first black pilot and commander. Gregory piloted the *Challenger* in 1985, and later commanded the *Discovery* crew in 1990. A veteran with two Distinguished Flying Crosses and sixteen Air Medals, he became NASA's first African American Associate Administrator for the Office of Space Flight in 2002.

Charles F. Bolden was pilot of the *Discovery* in 1990, and helped launch the Hubble telescope. This Brigadier General from South Carolina has logged more than sixty-eight hours in space. He also piloted *Atlantis* and *Columbia* in his career above the stratosphere.

Mae Jemison was an Alabama girl who grew up to become a Peace Corps Volunteer and earn a Medical Degree from Cornell University. Jemison became the first black woman in space when she flew on board the *Endeavor* in 1992. She conducted zero gravity tests aboard the first Japanese/American co-sponsored flight.

The first black man to spacewalk was **Dr. Bernard A. Harris,** when he flew with the *Discovery* crew that rendezvoused with the Mir space station in 1995. A former physician at the Mayo Clinic and a 1993 Physician of the Year, he flew on two shuttle flights and Spacelab.

Navy **Captain Winston Scott** has completed three spacewalks aboard the *Endeavor* and *Columbia*. Scott is also a jazz trumpeter and second-degree karate black belt, and has more than 4,000 hours of flying time in over twenty different civilian and military aircraft.

The *Columbia* shuttle crash of 2003 killed **Michael Anderson,** an accomplished physicist and a veteran of the Russian Mir space program. He was payload specialist aboard the shuttle, and was excited about the shuttle crew's test regarding treatment for prostate cancer, a common ailment for black men.

The new generation of black astronauts includes **Robert L. Curbeam Jr.,** a native Baltimorean with two Navy Commendation Awards. Curbeam flew aboard the *Discovery* in 1995 and operated the shuttle's robotic arm. **Ms. Joan Higginbotham,** a native Chicagoan who is a bodybuilder and a *Columbia* astronaut, became NASA's lead for Orbital Experiments in 1988. **Michael P. Anderson,** a chess player from Washington, flew aboard the *Endeavor* in 1998. Waiting in the wings are **Dr. Stephanie Wilson** and **Dr. Yvonne Cagle,** who have both completed their astronaut training.

Astronaut training is a highly rigorous program that very few are able to conquer. Those who complete the training are highly skilled in sciences, physics, piloting, medicine, and other sciences. The handful of black astronauts depicted here is a courageous lot, an elite club that is sure to grow with time.

Books to check out!

Mae C. Jemison: First Black Female Astronaut by Eabraska Ceasor
Ronald McNair: Astronaut by Corrine J. Naden

Inventors: Black Genius at Work

Benjamin Banneker was born free on a farm outside Baltimore, Maryland, in 1731. His grandmother was Molly Walsh, a white indentured servant from England who, at the end of her servitude, purchased and married his grandfather, Bannaky. Bannaky successfully applied African irrigation methods to their farm. Their daughter, Mary, also purchased a slave and married him, and their child was Benjamin. Benjamin received a Quaker education, and excelled at math. When a traveler gave him a pocket watch, Banneker took it apart found out how it worked, and carved a clock out of wood that ran perfectly on time for forty years—the first clock in the United States. He later published the widely popular almanac *Almanack and Ephemeris* from 1792 to 1892. Later, he was part of the team that designed the nation's capital, Washington, D.C. He died peacefully in 1806.

Norbert Rillieux (1806–1912), a free black born in New Orleans, invented the vacuum pan evaporator, a device which gave us refined sugar.

Elijah McCoy (1844–1929) held over fifty patents, mostly involved in the lubrication of locomotives to keep them from breaking down. This array of lubrication devices became know as the "McCoy system." Locomotive's inspectors would often ask of the machinery, "Is this the real McCoy?"

George Washington Carver (1860–1943) was born a slave and never knew his mother, who was raided off his master's plantation. He was educated at Iowa Agricultural College and could have had a promising career there, but when Booker T. Washington asked him to teach at Tuskegee, he immediately agreed. While he taught local farmers the value of crop rotation, he invented peanut butter and 325 other products from the peanut. He also developed 108 applications for sweet potatoes and 75 products from the pecan. Carver's work in developing industrial applications from agricultural products derived 118 products, including a rubber substitute and over 500 dyes and pigments, from 28 different plants. He was also responsible for the invention in 1927 of a process for producing paints and stains from soybeans, for which three separate patents were issued.

Madame C.J. Walker (1867–1919) invented a conditioning treatment for black women's hair. The process included use of a shampoo, a pomade "hair-grower," vigorous brushing, and the application of heated iron combs to the hair. While she did not invent the hot comb, she did use the device to facilitate hair care. An orphan by the age of seven, and a widowed mother by twenty, she began selling her products door-to-door and became the nation's first black millionaire.

Majorie Joyner, an employee of Madame Walker's empire, invented a permanent wave machine.

Mary B. Kenner, a burn victim who as a teenager with other classmates, was instrumental in establishing Black History Month. Kenner was the most prolific African American woman inventor. She developed the Sanitary belt, the Sanitary belt with moisture proof napkin pocket, a bathroom tissue holder and a carrier attachment for an invalid walker.

Dr. Daniel Hale Williams (1856–1931) spearheaded the founding of America's first interracial hospital: Provident, located in Chicago, Illinois. He also performed the world's first open heart surgery on July 9, 1893.

Dr. Louis Tompkins Wright (1891–1952) was the first black police surgeon in New York City, a diplomate of the American Board of Surgery, and inventor of a neck brace and a special blade plate that was used for knee fractures.

Percy Lavon Julian was the "soybean chemist," a friend to sufferers of glaucoma and arthritis everywhere. He synthesized physostigmine for treatment of glaucoma in 1935. He also synthesized cortisone for the treatment of rheumatoid arthritis. He was the first black man to direct a major modern industrial laboratory when he joined the Glidden Company in 1936.

Dr. Shirley A. Jackson was founder of the first Black Student Union at Massachusetts Institute of Technology, where she became the first black woman to receive a Ph.D. in theoretical solid state physics. She worked at Bell Laboratories, the research division of AT&T. There, she explored theories of charge density waves and the reactions of neutrinos, a sub-atomic particle. Her advances in the field of telecommunications included the development of the touchtone telephone, the portable fax, the solar cell, and the fiber optic cables used to provide clear sound in overseas telephone calls. Her technical skills made possible Call Waiting and Caller ID. In 1995, President Clinton appointed her head of the Nuclear Regulatory Commission.

Sarah E. Goode, a Chicago furniture storeowner, was the first African American woman to receive a patent when she invented the folding cabinet bed in 1885.

Other black inventions include: **Granville T. Woods**'s Synchronous Multiplex Railway Telegraph that allowed moving trains to communicate telegraphically with stations; **Lloyd A. Hall**'s "flash drying" process; **Jan Matzeliger**'s shoe lasting machine; **Henry Sampson**'s Gamma Electrical Cell; **John Standard**'s improved refrigerator design; **Louis Temple**'s Toggle Iron Harpoon; **Nathaniel Alexander**'s folding chair; **Patricia Bath**'s major advance in eye surgery, the Cataract Laserphaco Probe; **Otis Boykin**'s electrical capacitor that is used in guided missiles; **Bessie Blount**'s portable cup for paralyzed patients; **George Alcorn**'s research in semiconductor technology; **John White**'s lemon squeezer; **Kevin Woolfolk**'s Hamster Workout Wheel; **Mark Dean,** who holds three of IBM's original nine PC patents; **George Carruther**'s far-ultraviolet camera and spectrograph; **Meredith C. Gourdine**'s forty patents in electrogasdynamics; **Valerie Thomas**'s illusion transmitter; **Natalie Love**'s T-top roof cover; **Ellen Elgin**'s clothes wringer; and **Madeline Turner**'s fruit press.

Black folks are inventive people with inventive ideas in all areas of life. Whatever will we think of next?

Books to check out!

Black Inventors of America by Burt McKinley
Outward Dreams: Black Inventors and Their Inventions by Jim Haskins

Pullman Porters and the Brotherhood of Sleeping Car Porters: Service, Not Servitude

The years after the Civil War ushered in the era of rail travel, a revolution in American mobility. In 1867, the Chicago industrialist George M. Pullman, founder of the Pullman Palace Car Company, set about hiring former slaves to provide service in the luxurious railway cars that he sold or leased to railroads. He believed they were "by nature adapted faithfully to perform their duties under circumstances which necessitate unfailing good nature, solicitude, and faithfulness." It was also a common saying in the black community that "Lincoln freed the slaves, but Pullman hired them."

A career as a Pullman Porter was fraught with contradictions. The pay was miserable—$27.50 per month in 1915—but the tips made the job worthwhile. Pullman men had to work hard and smile for their tips, taking advantage of white folks' feelings of superiority—but for a very long time they were well respected in the black community because of their steady jobs in an economy with few stable employment options for blacks. They were required to work an abominable schedule—400 hours or 11,000 miles per month—but they got to see many parts of the country, and served as a lifeline between black communities across the country by bringing big city news and music to small rural communities. When lynching was a scourge of the South, Pullman porters brought thousands of *Chicago Defender* newspapers down to southern small towns with news of the relative equality and job opportunities available in Chicago and other northern industrial cities.

By World War I, approximately 12,000 black porters worked for the Pullman Company. College graduates and third grade dropouts alike could be found riding the rails in a Pullman uniform. And while their beginnings were often humble, many used the jobs as a base before moving on to important roles in their community. Former porters include Malcolm X, Claude McKay, Benjamin E. Mays, president of Morehouse College, Perry Howard, Republican national committeeman from Mississippi, Jesse Binga, head of Chicago's Binga State Bank, and J. Finley Watson, Grand Exalted Ruler of the Elks. The most distinguished labor leaders to rise from the ranks of porters were **A. Phillip Randolph** and **Milton Webster.**

By 1925, a Pullman Porter's salary averaged $810 per year—less than $8,000 in today's economy. At the time, there were over 20,000 black Pullman Porters and other train personnel working on America's railways. It was a prime time for A. P. Randolph and several other porters to found the **Brotherhood of Sleeping Car Porters** (BSCP), a feisty organization that fought against the paternalism of the Pullman Company for twelve years to become recognized as the porter's official union.

Because the Pullman Company had subsidized many black organizations and had started its own Employee Representation Plan to mollify attempts at organizing unions, the BSCP had to work closely within the black community in order to persuade them to take the risk of organizing. Women's club members such as **Ida B. Wells** often worked with them in order to create an overpowering movement that acknowledged social as well as labor goals for the black community. The **Ladies Auxiliary of the BSCP** and the **BSCP Citizen's Committee** organized many porters' wives and families into a coherent movement that was active in political action throughout the late 20s and 30s.

Finally, in 1934, a Railway Labor Act required representation for porters. By 1935, the BSCP had received a charter from the American Federation of Labor. After twelve years of negotiation, the Pullman Company officially recognized the BSCP as the Porter's official union on August 27, 1935. The BSCP won an increased wage package and a reduction in the work month from 400 to 240 hours per month. It was the first time a major corporation had negotiated a contract with a black union.

In 1936, the BSCP was instrumental in forming the **National Negro Convention,** which organized **March On Washington Movement** (MOWM), a plan to bring about enforcement of Executive Order 8802, President Franklin Roosevelt's proclamation that eliminated discrimination in defense industries and government. The BSCP used its monthly newsletter, the *Black Worker*, to spread the news about its **"Double V"** slogan, "Winning Democracy for the Negro is Winning the War for

Democracy." While the plan to bring thousands of blacks to Washington was never implemented, the movement helped keep up the pressure to establish equal hiring practices in the nation's factories. The MOWM set the stage for another March on Washington that would take place twenty-two years later in 1963.

The BSCP took active part in American politics until 1969, a year after the Pullman Company went out of business and A. Phillip Randolph died. It is another fascinating jewel in the history of American labor and black struggle that an organization originally composed of former slaves became a leading progressive force for equality.

Books to check out!

Pullman Porters and the Rise of Protest Politics in Black America, 1925–1945 by Beth Tompkins Bates

A Long Hard Journey: The Story of the Pullman Porter by Patricia and Frederick McKissack

Those Pullman Blues: An Oral History of the African American Railroad Attendant by David D. Perata

SPORTS

Black Athletes: Elevating the Game Through Social Conscience and Superb Skills

Jack Johnson. Tiger Woods. Jackie Robinson. Michael Jordan. Venus and Serena Williams. Jackie Joyner-Kersee. It is impossible to read the history of sports in America without coming across the names of black athletes that have been so superb at their craft that they have elevated the game to new standards. Often, black athletes' achievements have been a source of pride for their community, particularly when sports were the only competitive activities in which the community was reluctantly allowed to participate. In a sport, there is no advantage because of skin color, and the results are clear for all to see. You make the goal or you don't. You strike out or you hit the ball. The net goes "swish," or the ball bounces off the backboard. You either knock a man down to his knees, or you get pushed around the ring. The same rules apply to everyone, and there is no hiding behind myths of intellectual or physical superiority.

Boxer **Jack Johnson,** who became the first black world champion in 1908, was reviled and scorned for wearing a grin on his face while he pulverized white men with his fists. He was outrageous, racing cars at top speed in his spare time and consorting with white women. It is not entirely accurate to say that he was an athlete of social consciousness, but his refusal to be anything less than what he wanted to be, his steadfast will to achieve his goals the way he wanted to achieve them, gave black folks pride, and perhaps allowed them hold themselves a little higher with each victory he notched on his belt.

In 1936, **Jesse Owens** won four gold medals in the Summer Olympics held in Nazi Germany, refuting Hitler's claims of white supremacy right under Hitler's nose. This man, who could outrun a racehorse, had set six World records—which also included 100-yard long jump, 220-yard, 200m hurdles—within a space of 45 minutes!

In that same year, **Joe Louis,** America's Heavyweight Boxing Champion, had twenty-seven straight victories when he entered the ring with Germany's Max Schmelling and was soundly defeated. Two years later, he knocked Schmelling to the ground in the first round, proving American superiority in the ring. He continued to reign in the ring for twelve undefeated years.

The **Negro Baseball League** thrived in America when sports were still segregated. When **Jackie Robinson** broke the color line with the Brooklyn Dodgers in 1947, he ushered in a new era of sports, and was voted National League's Most Valuable Player in 1949.

Niki Francke was the U.S. Fencing Association National Champion in 1975 and 1980.

Kareem-Abdul-Jabar—A center who grew to 7'2". He played for

UCLA from 1967–1969, and became the #1 1969 NBA draft pick. He played for the Milwaukee Bucks and the Los Angeles Lakers. NCAA Player of the Tournament (1967, 1968, 1969), NBA champion (1971, 1980, 1982, 1985, 1987, 1988), NBA MVP (1971, 1972, 1974, 1976, 1977, 1980), NBA Final MVP (1971, 1985), Rookie of the Year (1970). Kareem ended his career as the all-time NBA scoring leader with 38,387 points. Kareem started out as Lew Alcindor, and changed his name in 1971. He also provided an important cross-cultural connection when he appeared in Bruce Lee's *Game of Death*.

Arthur Ashe—The first black man to win U.S. Championship (1968) and Wimbledon (1975). He was also the 1st U.S. player to earn $100,000 in one year (1970); He won the Davis Cup as player (1968–70) and captain (1981–82). Ashe also protested apartheid in South Africa, and when he was diagnosed with AIDS that he had contracted during heart surgery, he used his celebrity status to heighten public awareness of the problem. He died from the disease on February 6, 1993.

Jim Brown—Here is a man who only played nine seasons for the Cleveland Browns but left a legend that has lasted ever since his retirement in 1965. He led the NFL in rushing for eight seasons, averaged 104 yards a game, and gained 5.2 yards per carry. In 58 of his 118 regular-season games he ran for at least 100 yards, and he rushed for more than 1,000 yards in seven seasons. He also ran for 237 yards in a game twice. Brown quit football in 1965 to make movies and work on race issues. He founded the Negro Industrial Economic Union to help black-owned businesses with technical expertise and counseling. In 1988, he created the Amer-I-Can program, a community effort to turn gang members into positive, jail-free, members of their communities.

Wilma Rudolph—This sister, who was born with polio and was told she would never walk, became the first American woman to set a world record for the 200 meter dash during the Olympic trials and then won three Olympic gold medals. On September 7th, 1960, she won the 100-meter dash, the 200-meter dash, and ran the anchor on the 400-meter relay team in the Rome Olympics. She was the United Press Athlete of the Year 1960 and Associated Press Woman Athlete of the Year 1960. Wilma insisted that her homecoming parade in Clarksville, Tennessee be an integrated event, and so it became the first mixed race event ever held in the town. The banquet held in her honor was the first time in Clarksville's history that blacks and whites had ever celebrated under the same roof. She also participated in organized protests to help strike down local Jim Crow laws.

Althea Gibson went from hardscrabble streets of Harlem to the clay courts of Wimbledon. Gibson was one of the leading women in amateur tennis during the 1950's. The 5'10" phenom broke the color barrier of the American Lawn Tennis league in 1956, and took both the French and Italian titles. Gibson became the first black player to win singles and doubles at Wimbledon in 1957. In 1959 she turned pro and won the women's professional singles title in 1960.

Ralph Metcalfe broke or tied every world record in races from 40 to 220 yards in track in the 1932 Olympics. He also won the 400-medley relay race with Jesse Owens in the 1936 Olympics in Berlin. From 1954 to 1970 he was Athletic Commissioner of Illinois. He was elected U.S. Congressman in 1971, an office he held until his death in 1978.

Michael Jordan played in 1,072 games, playing an amazing 41,011 minutes and finished his career with 32,292 points, 5,633 assists, and 6,672 rebounds. His 30.12 points per game career average is the best in NBA history. He was also five-time NBA Most Valuable Player and ten-time All-NBA First Team selection. In 1996, he founded the Jordan Institute for Families at University of North Carolina, Chapel Hill. His $1 million donation was the largest gift ever to Carolina from an active professional athlete. He also helped found the James R. Jordan Boys & Girls Club and Family Life Center on Chicago's west side with a $2 million gift.

Beginning in 2003, native African basketball players **Dikembe Mutombo, Ruben Boumtje Boumtje, Mamadou N'diaye,** and **DeSagana Diop** have served as coaches at Africa 100 Camp, an endeavor to coach basketball and provide educational programs that address important social issues for the top 100 young players from more than 19 African countries.

Tiger Woods, the young black man who single handedly changed the face of golf, started the Tiger Woods Foundation. Through this organization, he has been able to contribute to 159 programs in 91 cities in 32 states through golf programs for youth of color and donations to community programs.

The next frontier for blacks in sports is ownership, management, and coaching of teams. Michael Jordan purchased the Washington Wizards,

John Thompson was coach of the Georgetown basketball team for several years, and Julius Erving was president of the Orlando Magic. The horizon of team management in black sports has only begun to unfold.

Books to check out!

African-American Sports Greats: A Biographical Dictionary by David L. Porter
A Hard Road to Glory: The History of the African-American Athlete by Arthur Ashe

The Negro Baseball Leagues

While we often hear a lot about the major league baseball heroes like Babe Ruth and Ty Cobb, it's rare that we hear about the other league that existed at the same time—the Negro Baseball League. In another America, teams played under names like **Cleveland Buckeyes, Pittsburgh Crawfords, Memphis Red Sox, Newark Eagles, Baltimore Elite Giants, Kansas City Monarchs,** and **Birmingham Black Barons.** They were the teams of the Negro Baseball League: teams that often rated as well or better than many of the major leagues. Negro League teams were successful business ventures that gainfully employed hundreds of blacks and provided a huge source of pride and entertainment to the community. Without the accomplishments of the Negro Leagues, players like **Jackie Robinson, Satchel Paige,** and **Josh Gibson** would not have had a way to hone their skills and be ready for the time when segregation in baseball ceased in 1947.

At the end of the Civil War, baseball began to take its place as America's national pastime. In 1868, amateur white teams instituted segregation, but formal segregation in professional baseball teams did not exist until 1887. In the meantime, amateur black baseball teams barnstormed across the country playing games against other white teams or against each other. A group of New York waiters who called themselves the **Cuban Giants** formed the first professional black baseball team in 1885. A renowned batter, **Sol White,** played for the team and hit a .381 average in 1887. White went on to become manager of the **Philadelphia Giants** in 1902, and when he lost that year's black championship against the **Cuban X-Giants,** he hired their ace pitcher, **Andrew "Rube" Foster.**

Foster was a native Texan and eighth-grade dropout who rode freight trains all over the country to follow baseball games until he went pro in 1901. This awesome screwball pitcher, who won fifty-one games against five losses in 1905, became known as the "Father of Black Baseball" when he called together the owners of the best black clubs in the Midwest and started the **Negro National League** (NNL). This first all-black league featured Foster's **American Giants, Detroit Stars, Cuban Stars, Kansas City Monarchs, Indianapolis ABCs, Chicago Giants, Dayton Marcos,** and **St. Louis Stars.** Foster's team was usually a favorite, and consistently won with their hit-and-run bunt technique that frustrated opponents.

While the NNL served the Midwest, other regional leagues like the **Eastern Colored League, East-West League, Negro American League,** and **Negro Southern League** formed to serve the rest of the country. **William Augustus Greenlee,** a boxing promoter, numbers runner, nightclub owner, and WWI veteran, started a new Negro National League in 1933 during the Depression and revitalized the game. He also started black baseball's biggest attraction, the **East-West All Star Game** held annually at Chicago's Comiskey Park.

Some of the innovations that came out of the Negro Leagues include ideas that would change the game. Rube Foster created hit-and-run bunt play. **Willie Wells,** of the Chicago American Giants, wore a modified construction helmet to protect against bean balls—a predecessor to the batter's helmet. **Josh Gibson** hit eighty-four homers in 1936, compiled a .391 lifetime batting average and hit 962 home runs in his seventeen-year Negro Leagues career. **"Cool Papa" Bell** was so fast, he stole 175 bases in less than 200 games. The Kansas City Monarchs, home to a young **Jackie Robinson** before the Brooklyn Dodgers recruited him and broke the color line in 1945, played the first regular night games with a portable lighting system in 1930. Monarch player, **Satchel Paige,** pitched the Monarchs to four consecutive Negro American League Pennants (1939-42). He became the oldest rookie ever to play in the major leagues when he joined the Cleveland Indians in 1948, the same year the New York Giants signed **Monte Irvin,** who went on to hit .312 and steal home against the Yankees in 1951. These recruits were the beginning of the demise of the Negro Leagues, as more and more black players went to the higher pay and notoriety of the major leagues. The last Negro League games were played in 1961.

Cooperstown's Baseball Hall of Fame has slowly added only sixteen famous Negro Leaguers to its roster as of 2003. However, Kansas City, the birthplace of the first Negro National League, opened the **Negro Leagues Baseball Museum** in 1991. It is important to remember that from 1900 to 1950, there were 436 interracial games. The black baseball teams won 268 of them. The Negro Leagues were another example of black self-determination that rose above discrimination.

Books to check out!

Encyclopedia of Negro League Baseball by Thom Loverro
Cool Papas and Double Duties: The All-time Greats of the Negro Leagues by
    William F. McNeil

The Colored Speedway Association and Blacks in Motorsports: Beyond the White Line

Charlie Wiggins was an Evansville, Indiana shoeshine boy who could diagnose an engine problem just by listening to it's sputters, clicks, and coughs. His mechanical expertise impressed one of his shoeshine customers, Henry J. Benninghof, part owner of Benninghof-Nolan Company, an auto distributor and repair shop. The owner hired him to apprentice in his garage, where he eventually became chief mechanic. In 1922, he moved to Indianapolis and became head mechanic for another garage owned by Louis Sagalowky, who let him use part of the garage to build his own car, the "Wiggins Special," during his personal time. He was planning to barnstorm around the country like his contemporary **"Rajo Jack."**

The American Automobile Association had banned black drivers from its events, particularly after the flamboyant boxer **Jack Johnson** raced in an unsanctioned event against Barney Oldfield, the country's top white AAA driver, in 1910. Thus, there was no chance that Wiggins would compete in the white-only Indianapolis 500. In the meantime, however, several Indiana black and white business leaders such as

William Rucker, Oscar Schilling, Harry Dunnington, George LeMon, Earnest Butler, Alvin Smith, and Harry Earl started the Colored Speedway Association. The CSA sponsored the first Gold and Glory Sweepstakes race, which was held at the Indiana State Fairgrounds on August 2, 1924 and won by Malcolm Hammon, a local chauffeur. The 100 mile race attracted 12,000 spectators, and highlighted the careers of several magnificent drivers. Gold and Glory competitors were William Walthall, mechanic for the American Giants black baseball team; William "Wild Bill" Jeffries, a Chicago real estate mogul who went on to found the Chicago Colored Speedway Association, and Bob Wallace, who was so light skinned that he often passed for white in AAA races.

Wiggins entered the race in 1925 and won fifth place, but then won in 1926 and 1931–3, giving him the most championships of all. The race was a tradition that would last for a dozen years until 1936, when a pileup on the course took away Wiggins' leg and one eye, ending his racing career. Nevertheless, he had been able to start the Colored Race Driver's Association in 1932, and mentored several drivers, including Sumner "Red" Oliver, who became the first black Indy 500 mechanic in 1973, and Joie Ray, who became the first black driver to earn an AAA license to compete in sanctioned races in 1946.

"Rajo Jack," one of the first black racecar drivers, was born either Jack DeSota or Dewey Gatson on July 28, 1905 in Tyler, Texas. He started working for the Doc Marcell Mineral Show when he was about sixteen, working his way from roustabout to head mechanic for the fleet of twenty cars and trucks. He got his nickname from his side business, selling Rajo performance heads for Model A Fords. In 1923, he started racing and winning in everything from Model Ts and stockcars to midgets and motorcycles. He raced for forty years, barnstorming around the country in the "outlaw" circuit where they would let blacks compete. Even after he lost an eye in a 1938 motorcycle accident, he won two 1954 AAA events in Honolulu. He was inducted into the West Coast Stock Car Hall Of Fame on July 25, 2003.

Wendell Oliver Scott was the only black to win a major-league NASCAR race. Born August 28, 1921, in Danville Ohio's "Crooktown" section, he was a taxi driver by day and a moonshine runner by night, two occupations that demanded driving nerves of steel and mechanical knowledge. He started racing at the Danville Fairgrounds Speedway, and won 120 races in lower divisions. In 1959, he won 22 races, capturing the Richmond track championship as well as the Virginia State Sportsman title. Two years later, in 1961, he raced a car on NASCAR's top-level Grand National circuit. He won his only major race, a 100-mile event on a half-mile track in Jacksonville, Florida, on December 1, 1963. From 1961 through the early 1970s, Scott raced in nearly 500 races in NASCAR's top division. During that time, he finished in the top ten 147 times. In 1973, a crash at Talladega race course ended his racing career, and his story was told in the 1977 movie "Greased Lightning," which starred Richard Pryor. In 1999 he was inducted into the International Motorsports Hall of Fame.

Willie T. Ribbs, born in San Jose, California in 1956, began racing right after his 1975 high school graduation. He drove Formula Ford Cars in Europe and won the Dunlop Championship his first year. In

1983, he won five races in the SCCA Trans-Am and was Pro Rookie of the Year. In 1990, Willy ran his first CART Indy race at Long Beach. He ran in ten races and got two top-tens. He became the first African American to qualify for the Indianapolis 500 in 1991, and qualified again in 1993. In 2001, with the support of Dodge, he joined the NASCAR Craftsman Truck Series.

George Mack, from Hollywood, California, won International Karting Federation Grand National Championship in 1994. He also finished 16th in the Indy Racing League's 2002 IndyCar Series competition.

Herbie Bagwell Jr. has posted five finishes in the top five at Waterford Hills race course. He earned six pole position slots and two wins at Lime Rock in a Lola Ford. Additionally, Bagwell boasts five consecutive poles, three wins and seven top tens in one season, as well as seven top five's and one win in a Porsche 911 at Lime Rock Speedway.

In 2003, **Bill Lester** finished tenth in the O'Reilly Auto Parts 250 at Kansas Speedway, the second highest finish ever by an African American race car driver in the history of a major NASCAR circuit series.

Black folks have always strived to compete in every area of American life. Our strive for excellence in racing is another reason to have pride in blackness.

Books to check out!

For Gold and Glory: Charlie Wiggins and the African American Racing Car Circuit. Todd Gould.

Re-Inventing the Game: Early Basketball Stars

Yes, it is true that Dr. James Naismith, at YMCA Training School in Springfield, Massachusetts, invented basketball in 1891. However, it is also true that black folks applied a genius to the game that reinvented it and elevated it to another level of physicality and competition.

Harry "Bucky" Lew became the first African American to play in a professional basketball game when he played for Lowell (vs. Marlboro) of the New England Basketball League in 1902. After the league disbanded in 1906, Lew organized his own team and played for another twenty seasons. **Edwin Henderson** and Cumberland Posey, were instrumental in introducing basketball to the black community. A graduate of Harvard University, Henderson brought the game of basketball to his hometown of Washington, D.C., and later bridged the gap between black YMCAs and club teams. In 1906, the Smart Set Athletic Club of Brooklyn was the first organized black basketball club.

HEROES/SHEROES

Muhammad Ali
Boxer

I am the greatest!

Engineer of the Rope-a-Dope. Magician of the self-named "Ali Shuffle." King of the Ring. Mighty Mouth. When **Cassius Clay** was born on January 17, 1942, little did the world know that the howling infant would become the loquacious poet laureate of boxing. When his bike was stolen at age 12, all he knew was that he wanted to get revenge on the swindler who swiped his Schwinn. He told a local police officer that he was planning to do damage to whoever had absconded with his property, and the officer offered to give him boxing lessons so he would be sure to exact the proper revenge. Young Clay took him up on his offer, growing more and more rooted in the rhythm of rumbling in the ring. Soon enough, he was first one in and last one out of boxing practice each day, practicing his footwork until it was blurry smooth as bird's feather in motion, beating the bags until his hands were strong as steel and faster than a python's strike. While he may have forgotten about the lad who looted his bike, slowly but surely, the rough diamond of youthful talent carved himself into a jewel of a boxer ready to leave Louisville sluggers and search out national quarry.

When he came of age in high school, he won the 1959 National Golden Gloves middleweight championship, and regained the title again in 1960. By that time, he was ready for the Olympics, where he won a gold medal before coming home to start a professional career. By 1964, he was ready to challenge the hulking reigning champion, **Sonny Liston.** Liston refused to give the youngblood a chance at first, and Cassius had to taunt him into accepting his challenges until February 25, 1964, at Miami Beach, FL, when Liston retired after the sixth round. Cassius Clay, the clear underdog, had truly shocked the world—but he shocked the world even more when he announced that he had accepted the teachings of Islam and changed his name to Muhammad Ali.

This young upstart was clearly too much. Not only would he predict the round of his knockouts, not only would he make up rhymes about his opponents' ugliness, but he would also forsake Christianity in order to embrace a rebellious religion of black nationalists, the **Nation of Islam** led by **Elijah Muhammad** with a spokesman called **Malcolm X.** Ali was arrogant, charismatic, defiant, and indomitable: he was just what African Americans needed.

In 1967, Ali risked his boxing career in order to make a stand on an issue of political, moral, and religious conscience. Citing his religious beliefs, he refused induction into the U.S. Army, which was deeply involved in the Vietnam War. He told the press, "I ain't got no quarrel with them Viet Cong." He was arrested, had his boxing license suspended and was stripped of the heavyweight title. He was inactive from March 22, 1967 to October 26, 1970, which many feel were his peak years.

While he was unable to fight, appealing his conviction and suspension, **Joe Frazier** muscled his way to the title of heavyweight champion. When Ali won the right to return to the ring in 1970, he had to work his way through the ranks, demolishing Jerry Quarry and Oscar Bonavena, before setting up a showdown with Frazier. Frazier, twenty-seven, had a record of 26–0 with 23 knockouts. Ali, the self-proclaimed "People's Champion" at 29, had a record of 31-0 with 25 knockouts. At Madison Square Garden on March 8, 1971, in an epic, bloody battle, "The Fight of the Century," Ali faltered for the first time. Frazier dropped Ali in the fifteenth round and won a unanimous decision.

Ali was shaken, but not deterred. He came back to regain the heavyweight crown in 1974 by facing a giant, **George Foreman,** in another epic fight held in Kinshasa, Zaire and billed as the "Rumble in the Jungle." Foreman, with a 37-0 record, was considered invincible—his devastating punches had lifted Frazier off his feet and sent him to defeat. Nevertheless, Ali had a plan. For six and one half rounds, he leaned on the ropes and took the awesome pounding of Foreman's fists, urging him on with taunts and jeers while the champion tore away at his ribs and arms with the heaviest fists known to boxing. Just when his corner men thought that Ali was through, when they were seriously fearing for his life, and when Foreman had pounded away all of his strength into Ali's bobbing, weaving frame, he lashed out with all his pent up fury and pummeled Foreman into a stunned puddle of confusion sitting on the canvass. He called the ploy his famous "Rope-A-Dope," a stroke of genius so obvious yet so unthinkable that it took Foreman by surprise and made him lose his title. Ali went on to defend his title throughout the seventies, facing both Frazier and Foreman again in dramatic trilogies. Ali won the 1975 "Thrilla in Manilla" against Frazier but said later, "It was the closest I've come to death." He reclaimed his title a total of three times by the end of his career, more than any other heavyweight in history.

He continued fighting until 1978, when he lost to **Leon Spinks,** finishing his career of sixty-one fights with thirty-seven knockouts, nineteen decisions, and five losses, one by knockout.

His indomitable spirit not only carried him through extremely rough moral decisions, but also allowed him to dominate in the ring. A man of constant faith, he resolved to never be beaten psychologically.

Books to check out!

The Story of Muhammad Ali by Leslie Garrett
Muhammad Ali: Heavyweight Champion by Jack Rummel

Byllye Y. Avery and the National Black Women's Health Initiative: Sisters in Care of Themselves

Health Care Activist

Byllye Avery is founder of The Avery Institute for Social Change, and the National Black Women's Health initiative. For over twenty-five years, she has been a health care activist focusing on women's needs.

Avery, born in 1937, taught special education to emotionally disturbed students and consulted on learning disabilities in public schools and universities throughout the southeastern United States. In 1970, after a marriage of ten years, Avery's husband died of a massive heart attack. Left a widow at age thirty-three, she vowed to make health a central issue in her community, particularly that of herself and those around her. Along with several other Florida women, she formed the Gainesville Women's Health Center and Birthplace, a freestanding birthing center where she provided seminars and workshops to demystify medical care and encourage women to participate in their own health care. The organization sought to provide prenatal care and respectful and comforting service to women, as well as empowering knowledge that would give them more control over their destinies.

Avery also worked as director of a Comprehensive Education and Training (CETA) program, where she began to see the health problems that besieged many of her young female clients. Hypertension, diabetes, sexual abuse, teen pregnancy, depression, and low self-esteem ran rampant among young black women. Compared to white women, black women have disproportionate rates of diabetes, cervical cancer, hypertension, lupus, and die earlier and more often of nearly every serious disease.

In 1981, Avery met with twenty-two women from around the country to plan the first National Conference on Black Women's Health Issues at Atlanta's Spelman College. It was at this meeting that the Black Women's Health Project (NBWHP) was established. The organization's first self-help group was formed in rural Monteocha-Gordon, Florida, and in two years, there were twenty such groups.

At the first National Conference on Black Women's Health Issues, held on June 23, 1983, the 2,000 participants adopted activist Fannie Lou Hamer's quote, "I'm sick and tired of being sick and tired!" It was at the 1983 conference that Avery's organization grew to become the National Black Women's Health Project. Soon after the conference, there were seventy-five self-help groups across the nation, each one meeting with about 250 women. By 1986, NBWHP started working with women in Belize, Barbados, and Jamaica. Soon, the organization began an overseas effort called SisteReach to include women in Brazil, Nigeria, Cameroon, and South Africa.

In 1990, NBWHP started a Walking for Wellness program to enhance consciousness about health problems and fitness in the black community. The program eventually expanded to eight cities, and 20,000 women have participated.

Today, NBWHP is the nation's preeminent organization dedicated to improving the health status of Black women worldwide. In 2003, the organization changed its name to the Black Women's Health Initiative. Ms. Avery has received some outstanding recognition for her work in health education: a MacArthur Foundation Fellowship for Social Contribution; the Essence Award for community service; the Academy of Science Institute of Medicine's Gustav O. Lienhard Award for the Advancement of Health Care; the Grassroots Realist Award by the Georgia Legislative Black Caucus; the Dorothy L. Height Lifetime Achievement Award; and a Citation from the President of the American Public Health Association.

Avery's latest project is the Avery Institute for Social Change. In 1999 she published an inspirational book, *An Altar of Words: Wisdom, Comfort, and Inspiration.*

Byllye Avery is a woman who has made triumph out of tragedy and served her people in a meaningful, original way. The National Black Women's Health Initiative is a powerful force in our community thanks to her vision and the vision of those who helped build the organization in the tradition of black-on-black love.

Mary McLeod Bethune
Educator, Organizer, Entrepreneur

"If I have a legacy to leave my people, it is my philosophy of living and serving."

Born on July 10, 1875, in Mayesville, South Carolina, to former slaves Samuel and Patsy McLeod, Mary Jane McLeod was the fifteenth of seventeen children who worked the cotton fields on five acres of family land known as the "Homestead." Fortunately, the arduous and time-consuming work of the fields did not hamper her learning, and she excelled in her schoolwork at the local Presbyterian school. She impressed her teacher, Emma Jane Wilson, so much that she recommended her for a scholarship to attend Scotia Seminary near Concord, North Carolina. She graduated in 1894, and traveled to Chicago to become the only black student attending the Moody Bible Institute. During this time, she visited prisoners in jail, giving them inspiration through spirituals and verse. She also worked at the Pacific Garden Mission, preaching to residents of Chicago's slums and serving lunch to the homeless. When she graduated in 1895, she resolved to start missionary work in Africa, and made plans to go there through the auspices of the Mission Board of the Presbyterian Church, but was told that there were no openings for black missionaries in Africa.

She returned to Mayesville to help out as an assistant to Miss Wilson for one year, and then was transferred through the Mission Board to teach eighth grade at Atlanta, Georgia's Haines Institute. The director of the school, an ex-slave named Lucy Croft Laney, was a graduate of Atlanta University and a trailblazing example for Bethune. Atlanta was also where she met her future husband, Albertus Bethune, a man who eagerly believed in her prophetic dreams and visions. They were married in 1898, and a year later their son Albert was born.

Mary believed in the power of dreams. It was around this time that she began to have "crossing the river" dreams in which various figures, including Booker T. Washington, would encourage her to cross a great river despite her fear. In 1899, her dreams came to reality. Reverend C.J. Uggans, pastor of the Presbyterian church in Palatka, Florida, called her to teach a missionary school in his town. The new family packed their bags and headed down to Florida where she started the Mission School and sold insurance with the Afro-American Life Insurance Company. In 1904, she was approached by Reverend S.P. Pratt to construct a school near a major station for the new Florida East Coast Railway, Daytona. On October 4 of that year, she started classes in a two-story frame structure of which she said, "I had no furniture. I begged dry goods boxes and made benches and stools; begged a basin and other things I needed and in 1904 five little girls here started school." Thus was born the Daytona Literary and Industrial School for Training Negro Girls, a school with a tuition fee of fifty cents per week. In 1906, she sold ice cream as a fundraiser to buy the cheapest land she could find, a garbage dump called Hell's Hole, and organize its cleanup. Hell's Hole became the site of the first main building, Faith Hall, completed in 1907.

Bethune's thriftiness and hard work rapidly expanded the college, attracting the attention of benefactors and even the educator of her dreams, Booker T. Washington, who visited the school soon after its inception. Bethune College grew consistently to become a widely respected institution. In 1923, it merged with the Cookman Institute, a college for men, and became Bethune-Cookman College. The beginning decades of the institution were spent teaching on the elementary and high school level, until 1943, when the college established its first four-year degree in teaching education. By the time of the historic *Brown v. Board of Education* decision, the college had produced scores of young teachers to educate in the segregated schools of the south. Today, the modest beginnings in a $250 garbage dump have become thirty-five buildings spanning over sixty-two acres of land.

Bethune would be memorable if she had restricted herself to the colossal business of building the college where she served as president for over forty years. However, she had an important role to play in the women's club movement and the movement for civil rights as well.

From 1917 to 1924, she served as president of the Florida Federation of Colored Women, and in 1920, she was elected to the executive branch of the Urban League. During the Hoover and Coolidge administrations, she served on the National Child Welfare Commission. In 1924, she was elected to the first of her two terms as president of the National Association of Colored Women.

In 1935, she established the National Council of Negro Women, a coalition of women's groups that still exists today, with over thirty-eight national affiliate organizations and more than 200 community based sections. During the Depression, she also served in the Roosevelt Administration as the highest black government appointee of the time, director of the Division of Negro Affairs in the National Youth Administration.

Bethune retired from the college in 1948, but stayed active. She wrote a weekly column for the *Daily Defender* from her home and in 1949 traveled to Haiti to become the first woman to receive the Haitian Medal of Honor and Merit. In the same year, she traveled to Liberia and received one of Liberia's most prestigious awards—the Commander of the Order of the Star of Africa. In 1952, she cochaired a racially integrated forum called the Women for Peace Conference, and hosted it at the college.

Bethune died peacefully in her home on May 18, 1955. Her Last Will and Testament, which was published in *Ebony* magazine, was a poetic statement of faith, which bequeathed to all of us the tools for creating a better world:

> I leave you love. Love builds. It is positive and helpful. It is more beneficial than hate. . . .
>
> I leave you hope. The Negro's growth will be great in the years to come. Yesterday, our ancestors endured the degradation of slavery, yet they retained their dignity. Today, we direct our economic and political strength toward winning a more abundant and secure life.
>
> I leave you the challenge of developing confidence in one another. As long as Negroes are hemmed into racial blocs by prejudice and pressure, it will be necessary for them to band together for economic betterment. . . .

I leave you a thirst for education. Knowledge is the prime need of the hour. More and more, Negroes are taking full advantage of hard-won opportunities for learning, and the educational level of the Negro population is at its highest point in history. . . .

I leave you a respect for the uses of power. We live in a world which respects power above all things. Power, intelligently directed, can lead to more freedom. Unwisely directed, it can be a dreadful, destructive force.

I leave you faith. Faith is the first factor in a life devoted to service. Without faith, nothing is possible. With it, nothing is impossible. . . .

I leave you racial dignity, I want Negroes to maintain their human dignity at all costs. We, as Negroes, must recognize that we are the custodians as well as the heirs of a great civilization. . . .

I leave you a desire to live harmoniously with your fellow men. The problem of color is world-wide. . . .

I leave you finally a responsibility to our young people. . . . Our children must never lose their zeal for building a better world. They must not be discouraged from aspiring to greatness. . . . Nor must they forget that the masses of our people are still underprivileged, ill-housed, impoverished and victimized by discrimination.

The Freedom Gates are half ajar. We must pry them fully open.

Books to check out!

Mary McLeod Bethune by Eloise Greenfield

Mary McLeod Bethune and Black Women's Political Activism by Joyce Hanson

Anna Julia Cooper
Educator, Activist, Feminist

Only the Black Woman can say, "when and where I enter, in the quiet, undisputed dignity of my womanhood, without violence and without suing or special patronage, then and there the whole Negro race enters with me."

The quote above was taken from Anna Julia Cooper's classic book of essays, *A Voice From the South*, published in 1892. This seminal work marked one of the most articulate expressions of African American women's ambition at the time. Cooper was born on August 10, 1858, in Raleigh, North Carolina, the daughter of a slave woman, Hannah Stanley, and her master. When her mother was hired out to lawyer Charles Busbee, she was exposed to a wealth of literature and taught to read.

In 1867, she entered Augustine's Normal and Collegiate Institute in Raleigh, where she savored the education she received, but hungered to learn the ministerial classes reserved for men. She met her husband, George A.C. Cooper, and they married in 1867, and the two worked arduously together to achieve their goals until his death in 1879. Cooper persevered and traveled to Oberlin College in Ohio in 1881, where she had convinced the president to allow her to take the four year "gentleman's course" along with her contemporary, **Mary Church Terrel.** After attaining her B.A., she taught for a year at Wilberforce College before returning to Raleigh, where she taught at her alma mater, St. Augustine, for two years. She also helped found a Sunday school and a mission guild. In 1887, she began to teach at Washington D.C.'s M Street School.

By 1892, she had published *A Voice From the South.* This book, with its incisive analysis of sexism and its laconic tone, skillfully argued for the equal education of black men and women in pursuit of racial uplift. It is still a classic today.

In 1893, she was invited along with **Fanny Barrier Williams** and **Fanny Jackson Coppin** to address a special meeting of the Women's Congress in Chicago. She gave a special address on "The Needs and Status of Black Women in America" that impressed audience members such as **Frederick Douglass.** In 1897, she was the only woman elected to the **American Negro Academy,** founded in 1897 by **Alexander Crummel.** In 1900, she attended the First Pan-African Conference in London's Westminster Hall, where she addressed the issue of South African Apartheid. She also attended the Paris Exposition and visited the Exposition des Negres d'Amerique.

Upon returning to Washington, she became principal of the M street school. She revamped the school's high educational standards and progressive policies to an even higher level, and soon students were getting scholarships to prestigious schools, such as Harvard. Apparently, her incredible work raised the attention of the D.C. Superintendent, who was not pleased that the all-black school was outperforming other white schools in the city. The siege upon Cooper's ability to run her school effectively became known as "the M Street High School Controversy," and eventually Cooper was fired in 1906.

Cooper taught at Lincoln University in Missouri for four years before returning to teach Latin at M Street. Back in D.C. and over her personal half-century mark, she bought a house, adopted several children, and began to pursue her Ph.D. during summer sessions at "Le Guilde" in Paris and at Columbia University. She also applied to the Sorbonne in 1923, studying at the Library of Congress and traveling to France to meet her dissertation requirements. She became the fourth African-American woman to earn a Ph.D. in 1925.

In 1930, Cooper became the second president of Frelinghuysen University, a nontraditional school founded in 1907 by Jesse Lawson. The institution had many financial difficulties that hampered its survival, with Cooper even holding classes in her own home at times in order to keep the institution viable. However, by 1937, Frelinghuysen lost its charter, and was dissolved by 1939. She retired from teaching in 1942, but continued a public speaking career. In 1951, she privately published *Personal Recollections of the Grimke Family and the Life and Writings of Charlotte Forten Grimke*, her last publication. She died at the age of 105 on February 27, 1964.

Books to Check Out!

A Voice From the South by Anna Julia Cooper.
From Slavery to the Sorbonne and Beyond: The Life and Writings of Anna J. Cooper by Leona C. Gabel

Angela Davis
Activist, Educator

When one commits oneself to the struggle, it must be for a life-time.

Angela Yvonne Davis was born on January 26, 1944 to two teachers in Birmingham, Alabama. She lived with her family in a section of town called "Dynamite Hill," because of the bombings perpetrated by whites on black families to maintain residential segregation. Both of her parents were active with the NAACP, and taught their children to resist segregation. Because it was impossible to avoid segregated schooling in Alabama at the time, Angela decided to attend New York City's Elizabeth Irwin School at age fifteen. She later transferred to Brandeis University in Waltham, Massachusetts. Her course included a year at the Sorbonne in Paris. When she graduated *magna cum laude* in 1965, she spent two years at the faculty of philosophy at Johann Wolfgang von Goethe University in Frankfurt, West Germany.

On September 15, 1963, her hometown experienced an act of terror that would shape her resolve to work for justice: 11-year-old **Denise McNair** and three fourteen-year-olds: **Cynthia Wesley, Carole Robertson,** and **Addie Mae Collins** were killed when a dynamite bomb exploded at the **16th Street Baptist Church** in Birmingham, Alabama. Incidents like this and the many other events of the Civil Rights struggle convinced her to come back to the U.S. in 1967 and join the **Student Nonviolent Coordinating Committee (SNCC)** and the **Black Panther Party.** The following year she became involved with the American Communist Party. She also continued her education, pursuing her master's degree and graduating from University of California at San Diego in 1968. The next year, she became an assistant professor of philosophy at the University of California at Los Angeles.

In 1970, Davis was charged by the authorities with conspiracy to free George Jackson with a bloody shootout in front of a courthouse in California. She became only the third woman in history to appear on the FBI's most wanted list. The FBI claimed that Davis armed prisoners in the Marin County courthouse with guns that were registered in her name. After the warrant was issued for her arrest, Davis spent weeks evading police as signs started appearing across American in sympathizer's windows reading "Angela, sister, you are welcome in this house." She was later arrested in New York, and after a sixteen-month incarceration, acquitted of all charges in a heated and controversial trial. Because of her militant activities, the Governor of California, Ronald Reagan, vowed that Davis would never be allowed to teach in any of the state-supported universities. Upon release, she wrote *If They Come in the Morning,* an account of her incarceration that is still relevant today.

Davis went on to teach African American studies at Claremont College, and then to teach women's and ethnic studies at San Francisco

State University. She visited the Soviet Union in 1979 where she was awarded the Lenin Peace Prize as well as an honorary professorship at Moscow State University. In 1980 and 1984, Davis was the Communist Party's vice-presidential candidate.

In 1994, she proved Ronald Reagan wrong, and was appointed University of California Presidential Chair in African American and Feminist Studies. She is currently a tenured Professor in the History of Consciousness Department at the University of California, Santa Cruz.

Davis' work has contributed greatly to feminist and womanist studies, particularly her books *Women, Culture and Politics*, and *Women, Race and Class*. She has also been a steadfast critic of the Prison Industrial Complex, and has raised critical questions about the purpose of prisons in our society.

She has been featured in and written several books, including *Violence Against Women and the Ongoing Challenge to Racism, An Autobiography, The Angela Y. Davis Reader, Blues Legacies and Black Women, Are Prisons Obsolete?* and *Global Critical Race Feminism: An International Reader.*

Frederick Douglass
Abolitionist, Feminist, Publisher, Ambassador

I will not retreat a single inch—AND I WILL BE HEARD

Frederick Douglass was one of the most important abolitionists and the most influential African American in the thirty years following the Civil War.

Frederick Baily was born to a slave, Harriet Baily, and her white master, Aaron Anthony, in February 1818 on Maryland's Eastern Shore near the town of Easton. His earliest memories were of slavery: being fed at a trough with other children like pigs; seeing his grandmother stripped to the waist and whipped; wearing nothing but a dirty linen shirt throughout childhood; being separated from his mother by the age of seven.

By the time he was eight, he was given a chance to be a house servant for a friend of the Anthony's, Hugh and Sophia Auld. Frederick jumped at the chance, and soon found himself in Baltimore attending to the couple's child and running simple errands. Sophia Auld took a liking to Frederick and started teaching him to read until her husband furiously intervened, warning her that it was illegal to teach literacy to slaves and that it would discourage Frederick's obedience. Fred heard Mr. Auld's rationale, and decided straightaway that if white folks didn't want him to read, then that was what he would pursue. He covertly continued his lessons, paying local white boys with food, or tricking them into tutoring him. He eventually bought a copy of *The Columbian Orator,* a collection of speeches and essays by George Washington, Ben Franklin, Milton, Socrates, and Cicero, as well as heroic poetry and dramatic dialogues dealing with liberty, democracy, and courage. This primary source, combined with the mentorship of Charles Lawson, a local black preacher, and Frederick's nimble young mind, provided the basis for his stunning abilities as a public speaker, as well as his unshakable logic in matters of truth and justice. He would need this resolve, especially when he was sent to the Saint Michaels, Maryland, plantation fields of Auld's brother, Thomas in 1835.

Thomas Auld was an exceptionally cruel master who starved and beat his slaves. When Auld deemed the fifteen-year-old Frederick too uppity for his plantation, he sent him to Mr. Covey, a professional slave breaker who was adept at destroying self-esteem and resistance in slaves. Douglass, however, was not one to be "tamed." Rather than accept the brutal lashings that Covey gave regularly to his slaves, he escaped and took refuge in the woods. While hiding out, he met Sandy, a slave directly from Africa, who showed him a root that he guaranteed would protect him from further beatings. Frederick took the root, and when he returned to Covey's plantation and was attacked, he defended himself so well that Covey never tried to beat him again.

At sixteen, Frederick was sold to a farmer, William Freeland, who was much kinder—but by that time, Frederick had resolved to get free. He made another attempt at escape that was foiled, and was imprisoned until Thomas Auld bought him back and sent him to his brother, Hugh, in Baltimore. Frederick was hired out as an apprentice in a Baltimore shipyard, where he learned how to caulk boats. He eventually escaped from Baltimore, making his way to New Bedford, Massachusetts, where he was able to arrange the escape of his newfound fiancée, Anna Murray, from captivity in Baltimore. The two stayed in the house of Nathan Johnson, a free black man who helped Frederick choose an alias, Douglass, lest slave hunters discover him.

While Douglass worked in the docks of New Bedford and served as a preacher at the all-black Zion Methodist Church, he came across *The Liberator,* an abolitionist paper sponsored by the American Anti-Slavery Society and William Lloyd Garrison. He was enthralled with its message and eventually became a contributor. In 1841, his oratorical talents were discovered by Garrison, and from then on he was in demand across the country for his fiery and emotional skills as an abolitionist speaker. As his skills grew, some even doubted that he had once been a slave, a fact that prompted Douglass to write his 1845 autobiography, *Narrative of the Life of Frederick Douglass, an American Slave.* This document, written entirely by him and with an introduction by Garrison, is one of the most important accomplishments in American literature, and catapulted him into national prominence as a speaker. Its riveting story of privation and fortitude compelled readers across the nation and across the Atlantic as well.

Douglass continued on the lecture circuit and stepped up his abolitionist agenda when he began publication of his own independent newspaper, the *North Star,* whose motto was "Right is of no sex—Truth is of no color—God is the Father of us all, and we are all Brethren." When asked to speak at a Fourth of July celebration in Rochester, Massachusetts, in 1852, he declared:

> What, to the American slave, is your Fourth of July? I answer; a day that reveals to him, more than all other days in the year, the gross injustice and cruelty to which he is the constant victim. To him, your celebration is a sham; your boasted liberty, an unholy license; your national greatness, swelling vanity; your sound of rejoicing are empty and heartless; your denunciation of tyrants brass fronted impudence; your shout of liberty and equality, hollow mockery; your prayers and hymns, your sermons and thanks-givings, with all your religious parade and solemnity, are to him, mere bombast, fraud, deception, impiety, and hypocrisy—a thin veil to cover up crimes which would disgrace a nation of savages.

Douglass was not one to spare his words for any occasion. He was close friends with John Brown before his famous 1859 attack on Harper's Ferry. He saw the inevitable doom that awaited the effort and refused to sanction the violent expedition. However, when the Civil War began, Douglass recruited more than one hundred black soldiers from upstate New York for the Fifty-fourth Massachusetts, including two of Douglass' sons—Lewis and Charles. During the war, Douglass was an advocate for the Emancipation Proclamation—a document that President Lincoln was reluctant to sign until it seemed the Union would lose the war in 1863.

After the Civil War, Douglass continued in the struggle for human rights and women's suffrage. He was one of the few men to join the ranks of Elizabeth Cady Stanton and Susan B. Anthony in the Equal Rights Association in their appeal for women's voting rights. In 1872, Douglass moved to Washington, D.C., where he served as publisher of the *New National Era*, and in 1877, President Rutherford B. Hayes appointed Douglass with the largely ceremonial position of Marshal for Washington, D.C. Douglass eventually became ambassador to Haiti, and served out his term there until his death on February 20, 1895, from a massive heart attack.

Douglass' legacy as a tireless orator and champion of human rights serves as mold for those who wish to see an egalitarian society today. He struggled for freedom when it was not popular to do so, and never sacrificed his principles for profit. How can we continue his legacy today?

Books to check out!

Narrative of the Life of Frederick Douglass: An American Slave, Written by Himself

W.E.B. Du Bois
Sociologist, Activist, Scholar, Historian

The problem of the twentieth century is the problem of the color line.

William Edward Burghart Du Bois was a towering American intellect of the twentieth century. His scholarship informed and revolutionized sociology and political practice like none other of his time. His writings, from *Black Reconstruction* to *Souls of Black Folks* to *Philadelphia Negro* are critical documents in the analysis of class and race. His leadership of the **Niagara Movement,** the **National Association for the Advancement of Colored People (NAACP),** and the **Council on African Affairs** were watershed events in American history. His fervent adherence to social justice was unshakable, even after repeated harassment by McCarthy and the House Un-American Activities Committee (HUAC). He was a strong advocate of Pan-Africanism, the belief that people of African descent all over the world should unify for political power.

Du Bois was born on February 23, 1868 in Great Barrington, Massachusetts, and was so articulate that by the age of fifteen he was a correspondent with the *New York Globe.* He was the only black to graduate from his high school, and went on to attend Fisk University in

Nashville, Tennessee in 1885. There, he first became exposed to the realities of the Jim Crow South and gained resolve to combat the injustice.

Upon graduation from Fisk, Du Bois received scholarships to attend Harvard University. He defied a *Boston Globe* quote by former President Rutherford B. Hayes that there were no black students who could finish Harvard's advanced study abroad program at the University of Berlin. He sent his impeccable application to Hayes, who was director of a scholarship fund for blacks. Hayes denied he made the *Globe* statement and funded Du Bois' education. Du Bois went on to become Harvard's first black Ph.D. graduate in the social sciences, and his 1895 doctoral dissertation, *The Suppression of the African Slave Trade in America*, was later published as the first volume of the *Harvard Historical Series*.

In 1896, he taught at Wilberforce University, where he wrote *The Philadelphia Negro*, a seminal sociological work that, even today, serves as a template for urban sociology. In 1897, Du Bois began teaching at Atlanta University where he wrote 1903's *Souls of Black Folks*, a book of enthralling socio-political and personal essays that outlined his opposition to **Booker T. Washington**'s more accommodationist politics. Du Bois disagreed with Washington's agenda to create institutions that were concerned with only agricultural and trade instruction. Du Bois was concerned with another idea he articulated in *Souls*—the cultivation of a "Talented Tenth," a small (ten percent of the populace) phalanx of intellectually astute individuals that would lead the black population into equality and economic prosperity. "Mr. Washington is today the chief instrument in the hands of the N.Y. clique who are seeking to syndicate the Negro and settle the problem on the trust basis," wrote Du Bois. "They have bought and bribed newspapers and men." It should be noted, however, that Du Bois had congratulated Washington upon his 1895 "Atlanta Compromise" speech, and that the two were not completely personally or politically estranged from each other.

The following years saw Du Bois hurtling into action as an activist and deepening his scholarship with world-renowned research. In 1906, Du Bois called together a radical grouping of several other activist blacks on the Canadian side of the border to found the **Niagara Movement.** In 1909, the year Du Bois published his remarkable essay on a white abolitionist, *John Brown*, this grouping eventually integrated with whites and was the foundation for the NAACP. Du Bois became the Director of Publications and Research, and was responsible for *The Crisis*, the organization's magazine that helped launch the careers of artists like **Langston Hughes, Arna Bontemps, Countee Cullen, Jean Toomer, Claude McKay,** and **Alain Locke.**

Du Bois left the NAACP in 1934, and the next year published *Black Reconstruction: An Essay Toward a History of the Part Which Black Folk Played in the Attempt to Reconstruct Democracy in America, 1860-1880*, a volume that redefined the cause of Reconstruction's rise and fall. In 1919, he co-founded the Pan-African Congress, a series of meetings which would eventually serve as a breeding ground for future Pan-Africanist movements led by attendees such as **Kwame Nkrumah,** the first president of independent Ghana, and Jomo Kenyatta, of Kenya's Mau Mau movement.

In 1947, Du Bois published *The World and Africa*, his attempt to put the story of the black continent in a global context. He also became the leader of the Peace Information Center, an organization through which he demanded that the United States outlaw atomic weapons.

By 1951, however, the oppression of the McCarthy era had started to besiege the nation, and Du Bois was indicted under the McCarran Act for complaining to the United Nations about the plight of African Americans. While he steadfastly refused to bow under pressure to renounce his political views, his career and freedoms in the United States were jeopardized. In 1961, at the age of 93, he joined the Communist Party, and exiled himself to Ghana, where he began work on an *Encyclopedia Africana*, which would encompass the many accomplishments and histories of African peoples. He died there two years later, on August 27, 1963. Dignitaries came to mourn his passing from around the world.

Du Bois' quest for knowledge and freedom was completely unfettered by fear and driven by his tireless devotion to his sense of justice and integrity. We can only hope to be as devoted in our quest for fulfillment.

Books to check out!

The Souls of Black Folks by W.E.B. Du Bois
Black Reconstruction by W.E.B. Du Bois
The Wisdom of W.E.B. Du Bois by Aberjhani

Marian Wright Edelman
Human Rights Activist, Lawyer

Service is the rent we pay to be living.

Born on June 6, 1939, in Bennetsville, South Carolina, Marian Wright Edelman is a crusader for children's rights. With a father who was a pastor and a mother who was a natural born organizer, Marian was instilled with the values and talents that would serve her well throughout her life. Her parents, Arthur and Maggie, built a park behind their church to serve local black children because of the segregated public facilities in her town.

Wright attended Marlboro Training High School and then went on to Spelman College, an experience that introduced her to significant mentors, history professor Howard Zinn and Benjamin Mays, president of Morehouse College. During her stay at Spelman, she traveled abroad to Europe on a fellowship from Merrill Lynch heir Charles Merrill, another mentor she met at Spelman. The fellowship allowed her to study at the Sorbonne. While in Europe, she appreciated the freedom from America's Jim Crow laws, a new freedom that made her reflect that she "wasn't prepared to go back to a segregated existence." When she returned to Spelman, she graduated as valedictorian and entered Yale University law school as a John Hay Whitney Fellow.

By this time, in 1960, Marian found herself in the middle of a history-making epoch. She had participated and been arrested in an Atlanta sit-in, and had heard Martin Luther King, Jr. speak. She went to Yale intent on returning to the South to combat segregation. She left the dull confines of Yale to go to Mississippi in the summer of 1963 and work on voter registration with the Student Nonviolent Coordinating Committee (SNCC) and Medgar Evers. When she graduated from Yale in 1964, she immediately headed to Jackson, Mississippi as one of the first two interns for the National Association for the Advancement of Colored People's Legal Defense Fund.

During these dangerous years, Wright opened a law office to become the first black woman to pass the Mississippi bar, worked on several school desegregation cases, and worked alongside civil rights soldiers such as Fannie Lou Hamer, leader of the Mississippi Freedom Democratic Party, and Unita Blackwell, the first black woman mayor in Mississippi. She also worked with SNCC organizer Bob Moses and Mae Bertha Carter, whom she represented in a 1967 lawsuit challenging Mississippi's segregation policies.

It was in Mississippi that Wright became engaged to Robert Kennedy's legislative aide, Peter Edelman. They both made plans to move to Washington, D.C. where she would serve as counsel for Dr. Martin Luther King, Jr.'s latest social action project, the Poor People's March. Wright had also received a Field Foundation grant to start the Washington Research

Project, a project designed to bring government services to poor communities. The two married in the tumultuous year of 1968, soon after the assassinations of Martin Luther King and Robert Kennedy.

In 1971, she also assumed responsibilities as director of Harvard's Center for Law and Education. By 1973, The Washington Research Project had initiated the Children's Defense Fund (CDF). For thirty years, the CDF has been the nation's leading advocate for children's issues. The CDF has led efforts to decrease teenage pregnancy, increase Medicaid coverage for poor children, and secure government funding for programs such as Head Start.

Wright Edelman became the first African American female on the board of directors of Yale University. She served on the Board of Trustees of Spelman College, which she chaired from 1976 to 1987, and received a MacArthur Foundation Fellowship in 1985. She has received honorary degrees from over thirty universities. In 2000, she received the Presidential Medal of Freedom, the nation's highest civilian award. She has served as a member of the Council on Foreign Relations, the American Philosophical Society, the American Academy of Arts and Sciences, and the Institute of Medicine of the National Academy of Sciences.

Ms. Wright Edelman has authored seven books: *Families in Peril: An Agenda for Social Change*; *The Measure of Our Success: A Letter to My Children and Yours*; *Guide My Feet: Meditations and Prayers on Loving and Working for Children*; a children's book titled *Stand for Children*; *Lanterns: A Memoir of Mentors*; *Hold My Hand: Prayers for Building a Movement to Leave No Child Behind*; and recently published in 2002, *I'm Your Child, God: Prayers for Children*.

Fannie Lou Hamer
Civil Rights Activist

I am sick and tired of being sick and tired.

Born to a family of sharecroppers on October 6, 1917, in Montgomery County, Mississippi, Fannie Lou Hamer was the last of twenty children—six girls and fourteen boys. She contracted polio as a child and was left with a limp; yet, at the age of six she began picking cotton to help the family. She later remembered that "By the time I was thirteen I was picking two and three hundred pounds."

Like many poor black southern children, Fannie only attended school after the harvest, which wasn't for very long. "My parents tried so hard to do what they could to keep us in school, but school didn't last but four months out of the year and most of the time we didn't have clothes to wear. I dropped out of school and cut cornstalks to help the family." And so, she dropped out of school after the sixth grade.

In 1944, Fannie married Perry "Pap" Hamer. The young couple moved to the Marlow plantation in Ruleville, Mississippi, where Fannie worked as a timekeeper and Pap continued to work the fields.

During the 1960s Fannie became interested in the civil rights movement. She got involved in voter registration when members of the Student Nonviolent Coordinating Committee (SNCC) and the Southern Christian Leadership Conference (SCLC) came to Mississippi. As she told it later, "One day in early August, I heard that some young people had come to town teaching people how to register to vote. I have always wanted to do something to help myself and my race, but I did not know how to go about it. So, I went to one of the meetings in Ruleville. That night, I was showed how to fill out a form for registration. The next day, August 31, 1962, I went to Indianola, Mississippi to fill out a form at the registrar's office. I took the test."

When Hamer and others from her city went to register to vote, they were asked to interpret the state's constitution in order to deter them from qualifying as voters. When Hamer flunked, they refused to allow her to register. On the return trip home, the police pulled over the bus in which she and the others were riding and arrested the driver for having "too much yellow" painted on his bus. When she returned home, her landowner told her either to stop trying to vote or leave his property—even though she had been there for eighteen years. Hamer chose to leave, while her husband remained on the property to continue working. She stayed with various friends and neighbors in and out of Sunflower and Tallahatchie counties, where night riders threatened her life and the lives of her hosts with bullets and threats.

In order to assist other blacks in the struggle to vote, Hamer became a field secretary for the Student Nonviolent Coordinating Committee (SNCC) and the Council of Federated Organizations (COFO), traveling across the South on voter registration drives. On June 9, 1963, during one of the trips to South Carolina, the bus in which she and other SNCC workers were riding stopped in Winona, Mississippi. When some of the black workers went into the "white only" waiting room, the whole group was arrested. While in custody, the police beat Hamer and other workers unmercifully. Hamer suffered extreme injuries, which bothered her throughout the rest of her life.

"Three white men came into my room. One was a state highway policeman. They said they were going to make me wish I was dead. They made me lay down on my face and they ordered two Negro prisoners to beat me with a blackjack. That was unbearable. The first prisoner beat me until he was exhausted, then the second Negro began to beat me. . . . They beat me until I was hard, 'til I couldn't bend my fingers or get up when they told me to."

SNCC lawyers bailed them out and filed suit against the Winona police. All the whites who were charged were found not guilty. This injustice made Hamer more determined to fight for equal rights in Mississippi. She is famous for the words she said when she awoke in the mornings, "I am sick and tired of being sick and tired."

Nevertheless, Fannie never gave up trying to pass the Sunflower County registration exam. In 1963, on her second attempt, Hamer passed the test and became a registered voter. In 1964, an election year, the first vote that this forty-six-year-old woman cast in her life was for herself, a candidate on the SNCC sponsored Mississippi Freedom Democratic Party (MFDP). At the Democratic national convention in

Atlantic City, Fannie Hamer and other delegates challenged the Party for not addressing the concerns of Mississippi blacks. Hamer spoke to the Credentials Committee during the convention about the injustices of the all-white Democratic delegation. In one part of the speech, she asked, "Is this America, the land of the free and the home of the brave, where we are threatened daily because we want to live as decent human beings?" A compromise was made in which two seats would be given to the MFDP. The Democratic Party promised never to have an all-white delegation again. Thanks partially to the courageous leadership of Hamer and her colleagues, President Lyndon Johnson signed the Voting Rights act in 1965, empowering federal registrars to register African American voters in the South.

Hamer continued to organize grass-roots antipoverty projects in Mississippi, becoming a sought-after national speaker, and working to unite the black and white factions of the Mississippi Democratic party. In 1965, *Mississippi* magazine named her one of six "Women of Influence" in the state. In 1968, with the National Council of Negro Women (NCNW), she created the Pig Bank, a livestock cooperative to help poor people in Mississippi get more meat in their diets. The next year she founded the Freedom Farm Cooperative, a project through which 5,000 people came to grow their own food and collectively own 680 acres of land. In 1971, she helped found the National Women's Political Caucus, and spent the rest of her life working on issues such as school desegregation, child day-care, and low-income housing.

Fannie Lou Hamer died on March 15, 1977. Many civil rights leaders and workers attended her funeral. One of the many who spoke at the funeral was Andrew Young, former U.S. Ambassador to the United Nations and Mayor of Atlanta, Georgia, who said, "Women were the spine of our movement. It was women going door-to-door, speaking with their neighbors, meeting in voter-registration classes together, organizing through their churches, that gave the vital momentum and energy to the movement. Mrs. Hamer was special but she was also representative . . . She shook the foundations of this nation."

Books to check out!

Fannie Lou Hamer: From Sharecropping to Politics by David Rubel
This Little Light of Mine: The Life of Fannie Lou Hamer by Kay Mills

Jesse Jackson
Minister, Activist

I am somebody!

Jesse Louis Jackson's legacy is that of Martin Luther King's immediate heir to the civil rights movement. There are many who have disagreed with his tactics and his politics at one time or another throughout his career, but the fact remains that when one looks back at the last thirty-five years of the twentieth century, it is impossible to avoid Jackson's legacy of constant agitation and institution building for civil and human rights.

Born Jesse Louis Burns on October 8, 1941, in Greenville, South Carolina, and taking his stepfather's last name of Jackson at the age of fifteen, Jackson left South Carolina in 1959 to attend the University of Illinois. He married Jacqueline Lavinia Brown in 1962, after transferring to receive a B.A. in sociology from North Carolina Agricultural and Technical College. While in North Carolina, he led several civil rights demonstrations and was arrested for disturbing the peace, the first of many, many arrests in the cause for equality in his long career.

He returned to Illinois to attend the Chicago Theological Seminary, and was ordained a Baptist minister in 1968. In the meantime, he had joined the Southern Christian Leadership Conference (SCLC) in 1965, working closely with Martin Luther King and **Operation Breadbasket** starting in 1967. Breadbasket focused on promoting better employment for blacks through boycotts and negotiations. Jackson stayed with Breadbasket after King's assassination, in 1968 until 1971, when he resigned from the SCLC and started **Operation PUSH**—People United to Save Humanity. Operation PUSH, along with the **Rainbow Coalition** he formed in 1984, were among the most powerful multiracial coalitions of the twentieth century. Proof of Jackson's incredible organizing abilities across racial lines were evident in his 1984 and 1988 Presidential campaigns, where he came close to becoming the Democratic Party's nominee. In 1988, he had an upset win in Michigan's primary, and over 1,200 delegates at the Democratic convention, second to Michael Dukakis.

In 1989, he moved from his home base in Chicago to Washington, D.C. where he has acted as an informal diplomat for the United States, winning the release of hundreds of foreign nationals being held in Kuwait by Saddam Hussein in 1991 and negotiating the release of three U.S. POW's during the war in Kosovo. He also served as Washington D.C.'s shadow senator in the 1990's. His crusade against the death penalty represents the new abolitionist movement in America.

Books to check out!

Legal Lynching: The Death Penalty and America's Future by Jesse Jackson
A Time to Speak: The Autobiography of the Reverend Jesse Jackson

Rhodessa Jones
Singer, Dancer, Director, Actress, Social Worker

I love women. In all their incredible, magical terror.

Rhodessa Jones is the originator of the Medea Project, a theater workshop that funnels the energy of incarcerated women into imaginative and groundbreaking onstage adventures. Her work with women prisoners has helped address the growing issue of women's incarceration. According to Human Rights Watch, black women are incarcerated at rates between ten and thirty-five times greater than the rates of white women in fifteen states. California prisons house the largest number of women in the U.S.

Jones was born in 1948 to a family of migrant workers with twelve siblings and a strict upbringing with demanding parents. By sixteen, however, she gave birth to a daughter, and faced the challenge of raising her child and pursuing an artistic career. She kept her head up and eventually joined her brother, Bill T. Jones, in San Francisco to form a theatrical troupe, the Jones Company. She also became the only black member of a feminist collective, Tumbleweed, where she learned a lot about dance but was still hard up for cash to support her child. She turned to dancing as a stripper in San Francisco's Tenderloin district, which gave her inspiration for her first production, 1979's *Legend of Lily Overstreet*. This first foray into "performance art" catapulted her into national recognition. She met saxophonist, dancer and actor Idris Acka-moor that same year, and eventually became artistic co-director of Cultural Odyssey, a company that has developed more than a dozen original works which demonstrate a vision of "Arts as Social Activism."

In the mid 80's, Jones received grants from the state of California to teach aerobics to women in the state prison system. She quickly saw that her students needed more than aerobics to deal with the realities they were facing in prison, and she changed the focus of the classes to include acting. She conjured up a performance based upon her observations of the women in prison, and produced *Big Butt Girls, Hard-Head Women* in 1989 at the Women's Theatre Festival. When she took the show back to California, she decided to work with inmates to re-produce the Euripides' classical Greek tragedy, *Medea*. The production, was inaugurated as "The Medea Project: Theater for Incarcerated Women," and has spawned twelve productions as of 2002. This unique enterprise allows incarcerated women to constructively voice their fears and exorcise their demons onstage, a therapy that has allowed many of them to cope with their incarceration and to prepare for their imminent release.

This ongoing project is an instructive and unique way to address the perils of incarceration in the African American community. Rho-dessa Jones danced, sang, and acted her way out of the dangers of single motherhood, creating an ingenious way for other women to achieve progress out of prison.

Books to check out!

Imagining Medea: Rhodessa Jones and Theater for Incarcerated Women by Rena Fraden

Barbara Jordan
Legislator, Activist

This country can ill afford to continue to function using less than half of its human resources, brain power, and kinetic energy.

Barbara Jordan, a black woman from Texas who always carried a copy of the constitution in her purse, served as the first and only black governor of Texas and the first black Texan in the U.S. congress. She was the recipient of honorary doctorate degrees from twenty-five colleges and universities including Texas Southern University, Tuskegee Institute, Princeton, and Harvard, but she never forgot her lifelong commitment to her beloved Good Hope Baptist Church and her people.

Jordan was born on February 21, 1936 in Houston's Fifth Ward, to Benjamin Jordan, a Baptist minister, and Arlyne Jordan, a domestic worker. She attended Roberson Elementary and Phyllis Wheatley High School. While at Wheatley, she was a member of the Honor Society and excelled in debating. She graduated with honors in 1952 in the upper five percent of her class.

She then attended Texas Southern University, where she double majored in political science and history and pledged **Delta Sigma Theta Sorority.** She was a national champion debater, and won first place in junior oratory as a member of the first debate team from a Black University to compete in the forensic tournament held annually at Baylor College. She defeated opponents from such schools as Yale and Brown and tied opponents from Harvard University. In 1956, she graduated *magna cum laude* from TSU and was accepted at Boston University Law School. She graduated in 1959, and taught political science at Tuskegee Institute in Alabama for one year before returning to Houston in 1960 to take the bar examination and set up a private law practice. While in Houston, she became the first Black woman to serve as Administrative Assistant to the County Judge of Harris County. Her interest in politics grew and she decided to run for office.

In 1962 and 1964 she ran unsuccessfully for a seat in the Texas House of Representatives. But she was not to be deterred. In 1966, she was elected to a newly drawn Texas Senate seat, making history as the first African American to serve in that body since Meshack Roberts in 1883. It was the beginning of an incredible career as legislator. Jordan was the first black state senator to chair the Labor and Management Relations Committee, and the first freshman senator ever named to the Texas Legislative Council.

In 1968, weeks after the assassination of Martin Luther King, Jr., Jordan delivered a masterful address to local newspapers entitled "Who Speaks for the Negro?" in which she answered her own query by stating:

> What does he want? He wants "in." The Negro wants "in." He wants you to hear him, understand his condition, He feels that if you do this—if you really listen to him as he speaks through his presence and understand his condi-

tion—he feels that you'll save him. And that in the process of saving him you will also save this country. And in the process of saving this country you will save yourselves.

By 1969, when she started her second term as Senator, Jordan had politicked and empowered herself into the inner sanctum of Texas politics, and was able to pass new minimum wage bills as well as a Workman's Compensation Act, which increased the maximum benefits paid to injured workers. Jordan was unanimously elected president pro tempore when the Texas legislature convened in special session in March, 1972. On June 10 of the same year, she was honored by being named Governor for a Day.

In 1971, she successfully negotiated a redistricting session that gave her a favorably drawn Eighteenth Congressional District in Houston. She decided to run for Congress, and in November of 1972 became Texas' first black representative in the U.S. House of Representatives.

Despite the slow onset of Multiple Sclerosis in 1972, a disease that eventually left her confined to a wheelchair, she continued on a fervent pace throughout her stay in Congress. She helped broaden the Voting Rights Act of 1965, expanding it to cover Mexican Americans in Texas and other southwestern states and extending its authority to those states where minorities had been denied the right to vote or had had been restricted by discriminatory practices like literacy tests.

At the 1974 impeachment hearing of President Richard Nixon, she became a national hero for her unforgettable speech where she intoned,

"My faith in the Constitution is whole, it is complete, it is total." before casting her vote for impeachment.

Jordan became the first black selected to keynote a major political convention when she appeared before the Democratic National Convention in 1976, an honor she was to repeat in 1992. President Jimmy Carter considered her for attorney general and U.N. Ambassador but she chose to remain in Congress until 1978, when she became ill and retired from politics.

She became a Professor of Public Affairs at the Lyndon Baines Johnson School of Public Affairs. In 1987, she spoke out against Supreme Court nominee Robert Bork. Later, she served as an unpaid ethics adviser for Texas Governor Ann Richards, and was praised for her work on President Clinton's Commission on Immigration Reform. In 1994, she received the Presidential Medal of Freedom.

Both as a state senator and as a U.S. Congressman, Jordan sponsored bills that championed the cause of poor, black, and disadvantaged people. Barbara Jordan died of complications from pneumonia on January 17, 1996 in Austin, Texas.

Books to check out!

Barbara Jordan: American Hero by Mary Beth Rogers
Barbara Jordan: The Biography by Austin Teutsch

Martin Luther King Jr.

Since his death, Martin Luther King Jr., has been written about so often, his words quoted so many times, his name used by so many political causes, and his identity traded upon in so many ways, that his memory has been turned into a political cliché. People invoke King's name when they want to uphold a banner of righteousness and equality whether they are liberals, conservatives, corporations, not-for-profits, folks of every faith and color imaginable, atheists, black nationalists, integrationists, feminists, or gays.

He has been called socialist, preacher, instigator, fool, a threat to national security, genius, troublemaker, capitalist, peacenik, anti-American, patriot, sellout, radical, martyr, dangerous, delusional, angel, and devil. He has been quoted in almost every language in every nation known to humankind.

There are many books and articles written about King, written from different perspectives and for many different purposes. This author would contend that the most important thing about Martin is that he dedicated all of his soul and put his life on the line for the idea of justice and equality for people of color and the poor, and paid the ultimate price for it.

He was born on January 15, 1929, the son of a father and grandfather who were pastors of the Ebenezer Baptist Church in Atlanta. Martin attended segregated public schools in Georgia, graduating from high school at the age of fifteen. In 1948, at the age of nineteen, he received a B. A. from Morehouse College. He then attended Pennsylvania's Crozer Theological Seminary where he was elected president of a predominantly white senior class, and was awarded a B.D. in 1951. He won a fellowship from Crozer to enroll in graduate studies at Boston University, where he completed his residence for a doctorate in 1953 and his Ph.D. in 1955. In Boston, he met and married Coretta Scott, and together they had two sons and two daughters.

In 1954, King accepted the pastorale of Montgomery, Alabama's Dexter Avenue Baptist Church. By this time, King was a member of the executive committee of the National Association for the Advancement of Colored People (NAACP).

In December, 1955, he accepted the leadership of the first great black nonviolent demonstration of contemporary times in the United States, a bus boycott begun by the collaboration of women such as the NAACP's E.D. Nixon, and Rosa Parks, who courageously refused to move to the back of a segregated Montgomery bus. The boycott lasted 382 days, until December 21, 1956, after the Supreme Court of the United States declared the laws requiring segregation on buses unconstitutional. During the boycott, King was abused, arrested, his home was bombed, but still emerged victorious.

In 1957, he was elected president of the Southern Christian Leadership Conference (SCLC), an organization formed to provide new leadership for the now burgeoning civil rights movement. Between 1957 and 1968, King spoke over twenty-five hundred times and traveled over six million miles, constantly putting his life in danger. Meanwhile, he wrote five books; *Stride Toward Freedom, The Measure of a Man, Why We Can't Wait, Strength to Love, Where Do We Go From Here: Chaos or Community?,* and *The Trumpet of Conscience.* He led a massive protest in Birmingham, Alabama, that caught the attention of the entire world, and inspired his "Letter from a Birmingham Jail." He planned drives in Alabama for the registration of black voters. In 1963, he directed a peaceful march of 250,000 people on Washington, D.C., and delivered his address, "I Have a Dream." He was arrested over twenty times, assaulted at least four times, awarded five honorary degrees, and named Man of the Year by *Time* magazine in 1963. In 1964, at the age of thirty-five, Martin became the youngest man to receive the Nobel Peace Prize. He turned over the prize money of $54,123 to the furtherance of the civil rights movement.

On the evening of April 4, 1968, while standing on the balcony of his motel room in Memphis, Tennessee, where he was to lead a protest march in sympathy with striking garbage workers of that city, he was assassinated.

King symbolizes the absolute best of African American traditions in scholarship, activism, and faith. If we are to make his contribution of soul and substance meaningful, should we not ask ourselves how we can dedicate ourselves to justice?

Books to check out!

The Martin Luther King Jr., Companion: Quotations from the Speeches, Essays, and Books of Martin Luther King Jr. edited by Coretta Scott King
The Assassination of Martin Luther King Jr. by Jacqueling Ching

Audre Lorde
Black Lesbian, Mother, Warrior, Poet

When I dare to be powerful—to use my strength in the service of my vision, then it becomes less and less important whether I am afraid.

Audrey Geraldine Lorde was born on February 18, 1934 in New York City, the daughter of Caribbean immigrants from Granada who settled in Harlem. She didn't speak until the age of five. At a young age, she decided to drop the "y" from the end of her name, one early sign of her fierce quest for self-determination, and began to read and write poetry. She said of her childhood, "I used to speak in poetry. I would read poems, and I would memorize them. People would say, well, what do you think, Audre. What happened to you yesterday? And I would recite a poem and somewhere in that poem there would be a line or a feeling I was sharing."

At the age of fifteen, she showed her teacher a poem about her first love affair with a boy in Hunter High School and it was dismissed as "too romantic." Because the school would not print it, Lorde sent the poem to *Seventeen Magazine* where they gladly published her work.

Lorde attended Hunter College from 1951 to 1959, and attended the National University of Mexico for a year, starting in 1954. She continued studying to earn her master's degree in library science from Columbia University in 1960, and worked as a librarian in New York public schools from 1961 through 1968. In 1962, she married an attorney, Edward Ashley Rollins. They stayed together for eight years in the 1960s, and had two children—Elizabeth and Jonathan. In 1968, she became the writer-in-residence at Tougaloo College in Mississippi, and experienced the virulence of the segregated South, an experience that greatly informed the political bent of her writing. She also met the woman that would eventually be her long-term partner, Frances Clayton, and published her first volume of poems, *The First Cities*. 1968 was also the year she received a grant from the National Endowment for the Arts.

In 1970, the year of her divorce from Rollins, she published her second book, *Cables to Rage*, and joined the English department at John Jay College of Criminal Justice. She received a received a Creative Artists Public Service grant in 1972, and published her third book, *From a Land Where Other People Live*, the next year. In 1974, *Land* was nominated for a National Book Award, and she published *New York Head Shot and Museum*. She went on to publish several highly acclaimed books of poetry throughout her career, creating a body of work that is considered among the best in American poetry: *Between Ourselves* (1976); *Undersong: Chosen Poems Old and New* (1992); *Coal* (1976); *The Black Unicorn* (1978); *Chosen Poems: Old and New* (1982); *Our Dead Behind Us* (1986); and *The Marvelous Arithmetics of Distance: Poems 1987–1992* (1993).

She also published several collections of essays that have been essential to the development of womanist and feminist critique: *The Cancer Journals* (1980); *Zami: A New Spelling of My Name* (1982); *Lesbian Party: An Anthology* (1982); *Sister Outsider: Essays and Speeches* (1984); *I Am Your Sister: Black Women Organizing Across Sexualities* (1985); *Burst of Light* (1988); and *Need: A Chorale For Black Women Voices* (1990).

In *The Cancer Journals*, which won the Caucus Book of the Year award for 1981, Lorde broke the taboos against women speaking out regarding the health of their own bodies and used poetry to chronicle her fourteen-year battle with breast cancer. Her decision to live without an artificial breast after her mastectomy enabled her to serve as a living critique of the sexist values and standards of the predominantly male, white medical profession.

Lorde was able to synthesize all of her identities into one meaningful force on the page. She summed up her perspective when she wrote, "I cannot be simply a black person, and not be a woman, too, nor can I be a woman without being a lesbian. I write for myself and my children and for as many people as possible who can read me."

In 1980, Lorde returned to Hunter College as professor of English. She also helped to start Kitchen Table: Women of Color Press in the early 80's. A woman of constant evolution, she redefined herself in 1982 with *Zami: A New Spelling of My Name,* a biomythography that explored her upbringing and the transformation of her political and sexual identity.

In 1988, *Burst of Light* won a National Book Award, and in 1991, she was named New York State Poet.

Later, toward the end of her life, she made her home on St. Croix, U.S. Virgin Islands and adopted the African name Gamba Adisa, which means "Warrior: She Who Makes Her Meaning Known." Lorde died on November 17, 1992, leaving a legacy of literary excellence and courage for all of us to follow.

Thurgood Marshall

Lawyer, Civil Rights Activist, Supreme Court Justice

None of us got where we are solely by pulling ourselves up by our bootstraps. We got here because somebody—a parent, a teacher, an Ivy League crony or a few nuns—bent down and helped us pick up our boots.

Thurgood Marshall is the most significant black lawyer of the twentieth century, one whose constant litigation on behalf of Civil Rights took him across the country in service of the NAACP Legal Defense Fund, and landed him in the black robes of a Supreme Court Justice.

Thurgood Marshall was born in Baltimore on July 2, 1908 to a schoolteacher and a steward, William and Norma Marshall, at an all-white country club. He attended all-black elementary and secondary schools. He continued his education with the original intention of being a dentist at Lincoln University, where he earned a B.A. in 1930 with his classmates Langston Hughes, Kwame Nkrumah, and Cab Calloway. By the time of his graduation, he decided to pursue a career in law and applied to University of Maryland Law School—where they denied him entry because of his race. Perhaps, in retrospect, we owe U. of M. a debt of thanks, for Thurgood was not deterred from his path, and applied to

Howard Law School, where he was accepted under the tutelage of Charles Hughes, the law school's energetic dean who wanted to create not just lawyers, but social engineers who would shape the country's opportunities for blacks.

Oddly enough, one of Marshall's first courtroom victories came in 1933, the year of his graduation from Howard, when he successfully sued the University of Maryland for their discriminatory practices in *University of Maryland v. Murray*.

Marshall then traveled to New York and became Chief Counsel for the NAACP. During this time, he argued case after case in town after town across the South, arguing against racial discrimination and often winning. This was dangerous work. There were times when he would win a case by the afternoon, but have to vacate town by sundown in order to be sure of his safety. He also spread the message of the NAACP across the country, building a constituency and recruiting people to its ranks. He was also busy building international ties. The United Nations and the United Kingdom recruited him to draft constitutions for the emerging African nations of Ghana and what is now Tanzania.

Marshall's ingenious leadership of the NAACP Legal Defense Fund led to legal victories such as *Sweatt v. Painter* and *McLaurin v. Oklahoma State Regents*. In 1954, Marshall's career would be defined by the hotly contested case of *Brown v. Board of Education*, where he argued for the right of black children to attend the segregated Central High School in Little Rock, Arkansas. This tumultuous case effectively overturned the 1898 Supreme Court ruling, *Plessy v. Ferguson*, which established the legal doctrine called "separate but equal." The case was another step toward the death of legal racial segregation, or Jim Crow.

By 1960, he had drawn the attention of President John F. Kennedy, who appointed him to the U.S. Court of Appeals for the Second Circuit. Here, he wrote over 150 decisions including limiting government intrusion in cases involving illegal search and seizure, support for the rights of immigrants, right to privacy issues and double jeopardy.

In 1965, President Lyndon Johnson appointed Marshall to the office of U.S. Solicitor General, where he won fourteen of the nineteen cases he argued before the Supreme Court on behalf of the government. By 1967, Thurgood Marshall had represented and won more cases before the United States Supreme Court than any other American.

In June of 1967, Johnson nominated Judge Marshall to become an Associate Justice of the Supreme Court—the first African American to serve in that position in the nation's history. Marshall served on the court for twenty-four years until his retirement in 1991, two years before his death on January 24, 1993.

Thurgood Marshall was another example of black excellence. Through a keen inquisitive mind, he was able to help change the nation's history and end the long night of American apartheid.

Books to check out!

Thurgood Marshall by Helen Frost
Thurgood Marshall: His Speeches, Writings, Arguments, Opinions and Reminiscences edited by Mark Tushnet

Adam Clayton Powell
Congressman, Reverend, Civil Rights Leader

The Negro race has enough power right in our hands to accomplish anything we want to.

Adam Clayton Powell was America's fourth black congressional representative since Reconstruction. He was also the first representative from the Eastern seaboard since Reconstruction. He served as chair of the House Education and Labor Committee, a body that was responsible for forty percent of all domestic legislation in the country. As chair, he fashioned or influenced over fifty pieces of legislation that tremendously influenced equal opportunities for all Americans: 1964's Civil Rights Act and Economic Opportunity Act, 1965's Voting Rights Act, the Anti-Poverty Act, the Minimum Wage Act, the Manpower Development and Training Act, the Vocational Development Act, and the National Defense Education Act. He tacked on anti-discrimination amendments, called "Powell Amendments" to practically every appropriations measure before the House. His legislation helped to ban poll taxes and outlawed race, religion, and gender biases in job hiring. His persistence and wile got black reporters accreditation to the House press gallery, black sailors promotion to midshipmen at the Naval

Academy, and black officials on the U. S. delegation to the United Nations. He was also one of the smoothest talking, indestructibly cool people to ever swagger through the hallowed halls of our legislature; a former preacher who drank whiskey, Powell made little attempt to cover his extramarital affairs, and was alternately reviled and respected for his ability to make things happen in the cutthroat world of politics.

Powell was born on November 29, 1908, in New Haven, Connecticut. His father, the pastor of **Abyssinian Baptist Church,** moved the family to New York City while Powell was still a baby. Abyssinian Baptist, under the direction of Powell Sr., was the largest and most powerful black church in Harlem.

Powell attended Townsend Harris School and then enrolled in the City College of New York for two years before transferring to Colgate University with the intention of going on to medical school. He graduated with honors from Colgate, but decided to abandon his thoughts of being a doctor and to follow his father's footsteps into the pulpit of his Abyssinian Baptist. He went on to attend Teacher's College of Columbia University for a M.A. in religious education.

During this time, he became more politically active. He led a protest against Harlem Hospital for firing five black doctors because of race. In 1932, he started a church-sponsored relief program providing food, clothing, and temporary jobs for thousands of Harlem's homeless and unemployed. By the late thirties, he had succeeded his father as pastor of Abyssinian, and was busy building its congregation to 13,000. He saw the sociopolitical potential of the large church base, and used it to found the **Coordinating Committee for Employment** to fight for equal access to jobs, urging his people to boycott and picket businesses that would not hire blacks. In 1941, he ran for New York City Council and became New York's first black City Council member. He began to publish a newspaper, *The People's Voice*, which served as a rallying point in his campaign for election to the U.S. House of Representatives in 1944, the first year of his thirteen-term appointment as representative.

Powell's role in the House was indeed illustrious, as one can see from the accomplishments listed above. He also had tremendous nerve. He broke the color line in the segregated House gymnasium and barber shop by strolling in and ordering service—because he could. He took his staff members with him to treat them to meals in the segregated House cafeteria—ordering them to eat whether they were hungry or not.

Perhaps it was his self-confidence, perceived by white congressmen as arrogance, or maybe it was jealousy over Lyndon Johnson citing his "brilliant record of accomplishment," that aroused the anger of his colleagues. In March of 1967, they expelled him for misuse of House funds—pocketing congressional employment paychecks to his wife and taking junkets abroad with female staffers—and contempt of New York court orders concerning a 1963 libel judgment against him. He fought the charges all the way to the Supreme Court and won. Voters overwhelmingly re-elected him in a special election in 1967 and again in 1968. He was seated in the 1969 Congress but fined $25,000 and deprived of his seniority.

By 1970, however, the people of Harlem were ready for new leadership, and he lost an election to Charles Rangel. He retired from Abyssinian Baptist Church in 1971, and moved to Miami, Florida, where he died of prostate cancer on April 4, 1972.

He was a flamboyant fighter who fought against the odds. He made rules and broke them, but in the end, it could be said that he tremendously benefited the cause for equal opportunity.

Books to check out!

Adam Clayton Powell Jr.: The Political Biography of an American Dilemma
    by Charles V. Hamilton
Adam by Adam, the Autobiography of Adam Clayton Powell Jr.
King of the Cats by Roy Haygood

Paul Robeson
Activist, Athlete, Actor, Singer

The artist must elect to fight for freedom or slavery. I have made my choice. I had no alternative.

Paul Robeson was an extraordinary twentieth-century Renaissance man who refused to compromise his principles. He was born to Rev. William Drew and Maria Louisa Robeson on April 9, 1898. A native of Princeton, New Jersey, his father was an A.M.E. Zion church minister, while his mother was a schoolteacher. When he was six years old, Paul's mother was burned to death in a fire.

At seventeen, Paul won a four-year scholarship to Rutgers, making him the third African American to attend the college. At 6'2", 180 pounds, he was a great athlete, and manhandled his way onto the football field past the threats of some white players, and was such a good tackler, runner, and overall player that he earned a place on the All American team 1917–18. Robeson earned fifteen varsity letters in football, track, baseball, and basketball. He was also elected to Phi Beta Kappa society, and was a star debater, a singer on the Rutgers choir, and 1919 class valedictorian.

Paul decided to attend Columbia University's Law School. He supported himself by playing tackle and end for the Akron Raiders and the Milwaukee Badgers, one of the first NFL teams. He met his future wife, Essie, when he injured his leg after a game. He married her in 1921, and she suggested that he try his hand at acting as a lark. He took the title role in *Simon the Cyrenian* at the Harlem YMCA. A year later, he made his professional debut in *Taboo*, and appeared in the British version of the same play (newly titled *Voodoo*). In London, he met his future life-long collaborator, Lawrence Brown.

When Robeson returned to the states, he tried to find work as a lawyer, and was eventually hired by Stroetsbury and Miner, a leading New York Firm. Nevertheless, he quit within weeks when a secretary refused to take dictation from him. He decided that his dignity would be assaulted less on the stage than in the court room, and appeared in Oscar Micheaux's silent film *Body and Soul* in 1924 before taking the lead role in Eugene' O'Neill's *Showboat*, which was a critical success. From then on, Robeson was as unstoppable on stage as he was on the football field. In a London production of *Emperor Jones*, he was called back for twelve ovations. He also recorded four albums of black spirituals with the Victor Talking Machine Company and gave concert tours performing spirituals with Lawrence Brown across the country. He went on to star in stage productions of *Porgy and Bess, Othello, Black Boy,* and *The Hairy Ape* and got critical acclaim, but was dissatisfied with the stereotypical nature of the roles. He turned to major film production in *The Emperor Jones* and *Sanders of the River*, but found that the films were edited to reinforce stereotypes of African people. Paul had some films that he deemed a successful portrayal of black people, such as *Basalik, Stevedore, Songs of Freedom, Proud Valley,* and *King Solomon's Mines.* However, films like 1942's *Tales of Manhattan* were edited in such a biased way that he decided to abandon any more attempts at film.

In the meantime, Robeson and W.E.B. Du Bois founded the Council of African Affairs for the dissemination of "accurate information concerning Africa and its people, and the strengthening of the alliance of progressive Americans, black and white, with the people of other lands in the common struggle for world peace and freedom."

Robeson traveled internationally and found solidarity with working people across the planet in England, Prague, Budapest, Vienna, France, Egypt, and elsewhere. In Spain, he rallied Republican soldiers against the fascists of the Franco regime. Of his 1935 trip to the USSR he said, "In Soviet Russia I breathed freely for the first time in my life." These sentiments were to cost him dearly towards the end of his career, as he was slowly but surely whitewashed out of the American theatre scene; but in the '40s he was still a genuine American hero, one of the most respected black thespians and singers in the world. He was considered such an American patriot that in 1940, he recorded the chart-topping "Ballad for Americans," a patriotic song that lifted national pride when performed on live radio the previous fall and is an American milestone today.

Throughout World War II, Robeson supported unions and black voter registration in the south while he toured with *Othello.* After the war, he started to gain more attention from the FBI, as they labeled him a communist sympathizer. In 1946, he testified that he was not a communist before the House Un-American Activities Committee (HUAC). Slowly but surely, venues and cities banned Robeson from performing in their spaces because of his political views. In 1949, eighty-five concert dates in the U.S. had been cancelled, but Paul remained defiant as he toured in Europe and told the World Congress of the Defenders of the Peace "It is unthinkable that American Negroes would go to war on behalf of those who have oppressed us for generations." As a result, blacks and whites denounced him to the HUAC, there was a riot at his Peekskill, New York Concert, and in 1950, his U.S. passport was revoked limiting his career and his voice to American shores.

But Robeson never bowed to pressure to renounce his true beliefs. When recording contracts dried up, he started his own labels, *Paul Robeson Sings* and *Solid Rock*. Throughout his career, Paul remained defiant and conscionable in his political beliefs. When the HUAC called him back to testify in 1956, he called them "the true un-Americans, and you should be ashamed of yourselves." Finally, he was allowed some restricted travel in 1957. The next year, he published his autobiography, *Here I Stand*. He took his last concert tour with Lawrence Brown in 1960.

Paul died in Philadelphia on January 23, 1977 at the age of seventy-eight. He was a shining example of a man who did not care about the expedient course of action—he cared about the right thing to do. In an age when many actors and singers are willing to compromise their people's integrity for a paycheck, it is important to remember this man who stood like a rock in a sea of troubled water.

Books to check out!

Here I Stand by Paul Rebeson
Paul Robeson Speaks: Writings, Speeches, and Interviews—A Centennial Celebration by Phillip S. Foner
Paul Robeson: Artist and Citizen by Jeffrey C. Stewart

Randall Robinson
Activist, Lawyer

Things are never what they seem. In any struggle over policy outcomes, we all know the tools of contest: position, publicity, money, celebrity, fear, and vulnerability.

Randall Robinson, founder of the TransAfrica Forum, has played a key role in worldwide human rights advocacy. His leadership and organizational skills helped to focus international attention on the role of international commerce in peace and justice issues, and was particularly effective in the mass movement for American corporations' divestment from South Africa. His marching, testifying, writing, debating, and repeated acts of civil disobedience carried the Civil Rights Movement's legacy of activism into the late twentieth century.

In 1941, Robinson was born to Maxie Cleveland, a high school history teacher and basketball coach, and Doris Robinson Griffin, a teacher and homemaker. His brother Max later became the first African-American network television news anchor.

Robinson attended public schools of Richmond, Virginia, playing on the Armstrong High School basketball team, winning a basketball scholarship to Norfolk State College in 1959. In his junior year, he dropped out of college and was drafted into the army, where he stayed a year before opting for an early discharge due to a hearing deficiency. He decided to head back to school, finishing his B.A. in sociology at Virginia Union, and continuing on to Harvard University in 1967. During his years at Harvard, he became more interested in international politics, and organized a South African Relief Fund. When he was awarded a law degree in 1970, he took a Ford Foundation fellowship to work in Tanzania. It was there that he determined that he could best create justice for Africa from his homeland, the United States.

Robinson headed back to Boston to work for the Boston Legal Assistance Project, a legal aid group that served the poor. After leaving BLAP, he worked from 1972 to 1975 as community organizer for the Roxbury Massachusetts Multi-Service Center, where he targeted Gulf Oil Company's support of Portuguese colonialism in Africa with protests, picket lines, and boycotts. In 1976, he moved to Washington, D.C., to work as staff assistant to Charles Diggs, U.S. congressman from Michigan.

In 1976, Robinson accompanied the Congressional Black Caucus to South Africa on a mission to pressure the South African Government to end apartheid. Their attempts at persuasion were rebuffed, and they returned to the U.S. with a resolve to organize consciousness raising protests and boycotts of the country. In 1977, Randall Robinson helped found TransAfrica, "a major research, educational, and organizing institution for the African-American community offering constructive analyses of issues concerning U.S. policy as it affects Africa and the Diaspora in the Caribbean and Latin America." Randall served as its executive director.

During his tenure at TransAfrica, he pushed the envelope of protest and pressure politics to achieve passage of the Comprehensive Anti-Apartheid Act of 1986, a measure that had built so much momentum in congress that it was able to override President Reagan's veto and affect the policy of the British Commonwealth and the European Community. This legislation sounded the death knell of South African Apartheid.

His politics were not to be restricted by partisan interests. In April 1994, Robinson put his life on the line with a twenty-seven-day fast in order to protest President Clinton's policies regarding Haitian refugees, who were being sent back to a vicious regime. His campaign brought pressure upon the Clinton administration to cease the expulsion of Haitian refugees.

In 1996, he protested U.S. trade inequities that favored megacorporations such as Chiquita Brands by dumping thousands of bananas on the capitol steps with the sign reading "Chiquita bought Clinton and Clinton Sold Out the Caribbean." The expertly coordinated protest gained needed national press coverage for the issue.

Robinson received honorary degrees from several universities, and many awards for his human rights advocacy: the Hope Award from the National Rainbow Coalition; the Drum Major for Justice Award from the Southern Christian Leadership Conference; the National Association of Black Journalists' Community Services Award; Africa Future Award presented by the U.S. Committee for UNICEF; the Humanitarian

Award from the Congressional Black Caucus, and another from the Martin Luther King Jr. Center for Non-Violent Social Change; and the Trumpet Award for International Service by the Turner Broadcasting System. Through continued advocacy and writings such as *The Debt: What America Owes to Blacks,* Robinson provides well-thought-out discussion of reparations for African Americans. His book, *The Reckoning: What Blacks Owe Each Other*, challenges black folks to work with each other in sensible, creative, and responsible ways to help each other achieve the best in our communities.

Bayard Rustin
Activist, Organizer

I believe in social dislocation and creative trouble

Bayard Rustin—the man called "Mr. March" by Martin Luther King for his critical role in organizing the 1963 March on Washington—was an openly gay, extremely dedicated organizer for human rights. He organized nonviolent resistance constantly throughout his life, engaging in demonstrations that resulted in over twenty arrests, beatings, years in prison, incarceration in a chain gang, and leadership roles in several organizations. He was also known to be a fantastic singer, and a marvelous wit.

Rustin was born in West Chester, Pennsylvania on March 17, 1912, and raised by his grandmother in a Quaker community. He excelled as a student, athlete, and musician, and left West Chester to study at Wilberforce University and Cheney State. He began his career as a social and political activist in 1937, when he took an activist training program with the **American Friends Service Committee** and moved to New York to attend City College of New York. While in school, he earned tuition through odd jobs and singing with **Josh White's Carolinians** and **Leadbelly.** He also became a youth organizer for the **Young Communist**

League, working on the problem of racial segregation and advocating an anti-war position. He severed ties with the organization at the start of World War II, when they abandoned their position on equal hiring practices in the military. In 1941, he joined the planning efforts of **A. Phillip Randolph's March on Washington Movement** to protest continued hiring discrimination. The threat of this march later resulted in Roosevelt's Executive Order 8802, banning racial discrimination in federal defense departments and contractors.

At the same time, he joined and became field secretary for the **Fellowship of Reconciliation (FOR),** an integrated group of pacifist activists in the tradition of Gandhi. With FOR, he toured the country engaging in civil disobedience by participating in sit-ins in segregated public facilities, while conducting **Race Relations Institutes** designed to facilitate communication and understanding among racial groups. It was at FOR that Rustin met **John Farmer** and white University of Chicago student **George Houser.** He helped them organize the **Congress for Racial Equality (CORE),** an umbrella group of progressives that challenged discrimination through nonviolent means.

In 1943, he received notification from the draft board to report for a physical examination for assignment to work in a Civilian Public Service Camp, a statutory requirement for those like Rustin who had declared themselves conscientious objectors. He refused to participate, based on his moral objection that "Conscription for war is inconsistent with freedom of conscience, which is not merely the right to believe, but the right to act on the degree of truth that one receives, to follow a vocation that is God-inspired and God-directed." On January 12, 1944, he was arrested for violating the Selective Service Act and sentenced to three years in federal prison.

While he was in jail, **Irene Morgan,** a twenty-eight-year-old black Virginian, sat down on a Greyhound bus seat and refused to sit in the back. When she was arrested, the **NAACP** took her case to the Supreme Court, which decided that the Virginia segregation laws were a violation of statutes regarding interstate commerce. As soon as Rustin got out of jail in 1947, he helped organize a **Journey of Reconciliation** with an integrated group of pacifist activists to test the newly changed laws. During the Journey, Rustin was sentenced to a month of chain gang labor in North Carolina, which he eventually served in 1949 and wrote about in a New York Post article entitled "22 Days on a Chain Gang." The account spurred an investigation, which resulted in the abolition of chain gangs in North Carolina. The Journey experiment was the model for the famous **Freedom Rides** of the 60s.

From 1949 to 1952, he coordinated the **Free India Committee**, which championed India's fight for independence from Great Britain, and consulted with **Gandhi** and **Nehru** during sojourns to India. He also traveled to West Africa to consult with **Kwame Nkrumah** of Ghana and **Nnamde Azikewe** of Nigeria, and helped organize the **Committee to Support South Africa Resistance** upon his return.

In 1953, he was arrested on morals charges stemming from a gay encounter with two men in Pasadena, California. Forced to resign from the FOR, the **War Resisters League** immediately hired him as Executive

Secretary, and he continued under their auspices for the next twelve years. In 1955, he worked with **Martin Luther King Jr.** to organize the **Montgomery Bus Boycott,** which forced desegregation of Montgomery's public transportation system.

Rustin went on to organize the **Prayer Pilgrimage for Freedom** in 1957, **The National Youth Marches for Integrated Schools** in 1958 and 1959, and was the Deputy Director and chief organizer of the **1963 March on Washington for Jobs and Freedom.** His attention to detail and diplomacy was essential in making these events run smoothly and efficiently.

In 1964, Rustin helped start the **A. Philip Randolph Institute,** named for his mentor. Through the Institute, he continued to push for social change. He took part in 1980's **"March for Survival"** on the Thai-Cambodian border, and co-chaired the **Citizens Commission on Indochinese Refugees,** a non-governmental advocacy group working to assist the refugee fleeing Vietnam, Cambodia, and Laos. In 1982, he helped found the **National Emergency Coalition for Haitian Refugees.** He was also Chairman of the Executive Committee of **Freedom House,** formed to monitor international freedom and human rights.

Rustin received numerous awards including The John LaFarge Memorial Award, The Murray/Greene/Meany Award, The Stephen Wise Award, and more than a dozen honorary doctorates. He died due to cardiac arrest on August 24, 1987 in New York City.

Rustin was unashamedly gay, unashamedly proud of his heritage, and an irreplaceable contributor to twentieth century progress.

Books to check out!

Bayard Rustin: Troubles I've Seen by Jervis Anderon
Bayard Rustin and the Civil Rights Movement by Daniel Levine

Sojourner Truth
Abolitionist

Ain't I a Woman?

Sojourner; *Because I was to travel up and down the land showing people their sins and being a sign to them.*

Truth; *Because I was to declare the truth to the people.*

One of thirteen children, she was born into slavery with the name of Isabelle Bonefree in 1797, in the Dutch colony of Hurley, in Ulster County, New York. She was the daughter of James "Bomefree" and Betsey "Mau Mau Bett" who were slaves of Colonel Ardinburgh, a farmer. Her first language was Low Dutch, and when she eventually learned English, she spoke with a Dutch accent.

After the death of her parents at age nine, she was sold for the sum of one hundred dollars and some sheep to one master, then sold two more times to a fisherman and a farmer by the name of Dumont. She eventually married a fellow slave, Tom, and had five children. During her time with Dumont, he illegally sold one of her sons across state lines, and the boy ended up in Alabama.

In 1827, the state of New York abolished slavery, but her master would not abide by the law and set her free as he had promised until she had spun 300 pounds of cotton. After spinning the cotton, a fall's harvest, she left the plantation with one of her children, and took refuge with a nearby Mr. Isaac S. Van Wagener, who hired her while she set about filing suit for the reclamation of her son, Peter. She eventually won her suit, and got her son back to raise him to adulthood.

Isabella eventually settled in New York City, working as a domestic for several religious communes, and experiencing a religious conversion herself in 1843. That year, she changed her name to Sojourner Truth and started a famous trek through hundreds of miles of forest, back roads, and city streets, proclaiming her gospel of religion and freedom. She bent the ears of whoever would listen to her tales of slavery and triumph over suffering, and was known to make many tears flow when she stopped at a church or a meeting house to give witness to her vision of truth.

After several months of sojourning and sermonizing, she ended up in Northampton, Massachussets, at the **Northampton Association for Education and Industry,** a cooperative community dedicated to pacifism, abolitionism, equality, and the betterment of human life. Here, she met fellow abolitionists **Frederick Douglass, William Lloyd Garrison,** and **David Ruggles,** and became a more outspoken opponent of slavery. In 1846, the Association disbanded, but Truth stayed in Northampton and dictated her memoirs to **Olive Gilbert.** They were published in 1850 as *The Narrative of Sojourner Truth: A Northern Slave.* The publication of her narrative made her a popular figure on the abolitionist speaking circuit.

Sojourner was also a popular advocate for women's rights, and is famous for a speech at the 1851 Women's Rights Convention in Akron, Ohio, where she blasted opponents to women's suffrage by declaring:

That man over there says that women need to be helped into carriages and lifted over ditches, and to have the best place everywhere. Nobody ever helps me into carriages, or over mud-puddles, or gives me any best place! And ain't I a woman? Look at me! Look at my arm! I could have ploughed and planted, and gathered into barns, and no man could head me! And ain't I a woman? I could work as much and eat as much as a man—when I could get it—and bear the lash as well! And ain't I a woman? I have borne thirteen children, and seen them most all sold off to slavery, and when I cried out with my mother's grief, none but Jesus heard me! And ain't I a woman?

Then they talk about this thing in the head; what's this they call it? [Intellect, somebody whispers] That's it, honey. What's that got to do with women's rights or negro's rights? If my cup won't hold but a pint, and yours holds a quart, wouldn't you be mean not to let me have my little half measure-full?

Then that little man in black there, he says women can't have as much rights as men, 'cause Christ wasn't a woman! Where did your Christ come from? Where did your Christ come from? From God and a woman! Man had nothing to do with Him.

If the first woman God ever made was strong enough to turn the world upside down all alone, these women together ought to be able to turn it back, and get it right side up again! And now they is asking to do it, the men better let them.

In 1864, she met with Abraham Lincoln in the White House, and he told her that her speeches had given him inspiration.

After the Civil War, she organized efforts to aid newly-freed slaves.

She advocated alongside Martin R. Delaney to establish a "Negro State" in the newly opened western states. Truth continued preaching and lecturing until ill health forced her to retire to Battle Creek, Michigan, where she died on November 26, 1883.

Books to check out!

The Narrative of Sojourner Truth by Sojourner Truth
Sojourner Truth: A Voice for Freedom by Patricia and Fredrick McKissack
Sojourner Truth: Ain't I a Woman? by Patricia C. McKissack and Fredrick McKissack.

Harriet Tubman
Abolitionist, Orator, Freedom Fighter

Never lost a single passenger.

Araminta Ross, a woman of pure Ashanti African ancestry, was born into slavery in 1820, in Dorchester County, Maryland. By the time she was five years old, she was hired out from plantation of Edward Brodas as a laborer. By her early teens, she was working in the field from sunup to sundown. When she tried to help a fellow slave escape at age fifteen, her overseer beat her and hit in the head with a lead weight—an injury that left her in a coma for several months and gave her blackouts for the rest of her days.

Harriet married a free black man, John Tubman, at the age of twenty-four in 1844. They remained married for five years until 1849, when Edward Brodas died and Harriet became fearful of being sold downriver, where slaves were generally worked to death in seven years. It was then that Harriet carried her very first passenger on the Underground Railroad to freedom—herself.

Through swamps and forest, under cover of darkness, Harriet made her stealthy way ninety miles north past the Mason Dixon line. Eventually she made her way to Philadelphia, where she got work as a dishwasher in her first job as a free woman.

Harriet could have stopped there, but she decided that her own freedom wasn't enough. She decided that she wanted to share the benefits of freedom with the rest of her family, even if it meant the risk of capture and perhaps death. She ventured back into the gloom and shadows of night to retrieve her most valued possessions—her family. She ventured back over and over again until she had freed them all, and then she decided that she needed to free any slave that was brave enough to step out on the trail with her. Time after time she dodged from shadow to shadow, safehouse to safehouse, in rain, cold, and night to pull a trainload of folks out of the clutches of slavery. All told, she ghosted back south to free more than 300 souls from the plantation. Along the way she became the living scourge of the plantation owner, with rewards for her capture climbing up to $40,000 by 1856. In 1857, she managed to make her most memorable trip when she managed to free her seventy-year-old parents and bring them to freedom in Canada.

She once told Frederick Douglass that she never lost a passenger, but it is true that there was the occasional passenger who wanted to jump off the track. For those who found that they were weak at heart and wanted to give up the arduous journey, she would coax and cajole along the way until all other options were gone, and then she would pull out her close and persuasive companion, the loyal six shooter pistol that she kept prepared for enemies and stragglers alike. She would tell them in no uncertain terms that if they did not continue their journey to the promised land of Canada, then they would most certainly go to the promised land of heaven before jeopardizing the Underground Railroad with their capture. This frightening bit of persuasion worked many times to keep the motivational wheels of her locomotive well oiled and speeding along the track towards northern liberation.

After freeing 300 souls from slavery, Harriet was not content to sit on the sidelines of the Civil War and watch the action of shell and shot and spilling blood go by without pressing herself into service of the Union Army. She volunteered as a cook, a spy, and a scout, going behind enemy lines to gather information. Even after the civil war, her good works continued, as she established the Harriet Tubman Home for Indigent Aged Negroes, and worked for the establishment of schools for the freed slaves in the South.

Tubman is another reason to remember how to surmount the difficulties of life by keeping one's eyes on the prize. As Tubman said, "There was one of two things I had a RIGHT to, liberty or death. If I could not have one, I would have the other; for no man should take me alive; I should fight for my liberty as long as my strength lasted, and when the time came for me to go, the Lord would let them take me."

Books to check out!

Harriet Tubman by Jill C. Wheeler
Harriet Tubman: Moses of the Slaves by Janet Benge

Booker T. Washington
Educator

There is no defense or security for any of us except in the highest intelligence and development of all.

Booker Taliafero Washington was an ex-slave who educated himself, became the president of a university, and eventually became the most powerful black man in America. His book, *Up From Slavery*, was his passionate call for black progress through industrial education, and represents the mainstream of ideological discourse and political action at the turn of the century.

Born a Virginia slave in 1856, Washington moved with his family after the Civil War to Malden, West Virginia, where he worked in coal mines and salt furnaces. It was then, laboring in the dirt and darkness of the mines, that he began "to envy the white boy who had no obstacles placed in the way of his becoming a Congressman, Governor, Bishop, or President by reason of the accident of his birth or race. I used to picture the way that I would act under such circumstances; how I would begin at the bottom and keep rising until I reached the highest round of success."

He decided to do whatever he could to make it out of the mines. He hired himself out as a servant to a very strict white woman, Ms. Ruffner, who was obsessive about cleanliness and order. After a year and a half of her training and compensation, and after acquiring whatever books he could and hiring tutors to teach him how to read, he resolved to travel to Hampton Institute, a new school for black students that was about 500 miles away. He used the little money he had saved to catch a train partway and to walk and beg rides the rest of the way in order to reach Hampton a week later with fifty cents in his pocket. When he showed up at the school dirty, ragged, and broke, the teacher was skeptical and hesitant to admit him. Finally, she asked him to sweep a classroom—Washington seized the opportunity, and cleaned it the way he had cleaned Ms. Ruffner's house. The teacher inspected the room and admitted him into Hampton—that cleaning had been his entrance exam. Washington was given the position of janitor to work his way through Hampton. Upon graduation, the president of Hampton, General Samuel Armstrong, asked him to go to Tuskegee, Alabama, and take charge of a new industrial school for colored people. Washington started out immediately.

When he got to Tuskegee, there was not much there but a few one-room schoolhouses and a few acres of land to work with. Nevertheless, on July 4, 1881, Tuskegee Institute started its first classes. By 1895, the institution had grown considerably, due to the help of northern patrons and Washington's pugnacious attitude in fundraising and institution building. Washington was very shrewd in the use of his assets, and was also able to get the students of the institution to learn construction by building the very classrooms and lecture halls in which their antecedents would take classes.

Eventually, the school had a sprawling campus and hundreds of students, along with one particular genius teacher, **George Washington Carver.** Carver's research developed 325 products from peanuts, 108 applications for sweet potatoes, and 75 products derived from pecans. Carver was also responsible for the invention in 1927 of a process for producing paints and stains from soybeans, for which three separate patents were issued.

In 1895, shortly after the death of **Frederick Douglass,** Washington was asked to speak at the Atlanta Exposition. His speech, known as the "Atlanta Compromise," launched him into national prominence as he asked blacks in the South to attend more to industrial education than to political organization. Washington admonished blacks to "cast down your buckets where you are" and trust in the South for social recognition and eventual equality.

> Cast it down in agriculture, mechanics, in commerce, in domestic service, and in the professions. And in this connection it is well to bear in mind that whatever other sins the South may be called to bear, when it comes to business, pure and simple, it is in the South that the Negro is given a man's chance in the commercial world, and in nothing is this Exposition more eloquent than in emphasizing this chance. Our greatest danger is that in the great leap from slavery to freedom we may overlook the fact that the masses of us are to live by the productions of our hands, and fail to keep in mind that we shall prosper in proportion as we learn to dignify and glorify common labour and put brains and skill into the common occupations of life; shall prosper in proportion

as we learn to draw the line between the superficial and the substantial, the ornamental gewgaws of life and the useful. No race can prosper till it learns that there is as much dignity in tilling a field as in writing a poem. It is at the bottom of life we must begin, and not at the top. Nor should we permit our grievances to overshadow our opportunities.

This "up from the bootstraps" ideology won Washington entry into the hearts and minds of America's politicos. Soon, whenever a black was considered for a major position in government or education, Washington was called for a recommendation. Thus, from 1895 until his death in 1915, Booker T. Washington was the power broker of the African American community. He was funded by Andrew Carnegie and John D. Rockefeller, was the guest of the Queen of England at Windsor Castle, and dined at the White House with Theodore Roosevelt and family.

Washington used each circumstance to his best advantage, and did what he thought was best for his people. During his tenure at Tuskegee, which was one of the bloodiest periods for blacks in the country's history, he spoke out against lynching. Washington's message is still relevant today. As we reach forward to attaining new educational heights, we look back to the lessons of Booker T. for practical guidance to our future.

Books to check out!

Up From Slavery by Booker T. Washington
The Booker T. Washington Papers, Vol. 1-14 University of Illinois Press

Muddy Waters: King of the Chicago Blues

Muddy Waters took plain old Mississippi blues out of the cotton fields, dressed it up in amplified bass, guitar, and harmonica, and moved it to the big city to strut its stuff. Born on April 4, 1915 under the name McKinley Morganfield, Muddy was raised on a plantation near Clarksdale, Mississippi. He started playing harmonica as a child. By the age of seventeen, he bought his first guitar for $2.50. Aside from occasional lessons from guitar legend Son House, he taught himself just about everything he knew. Muddy's strumming got so smooth that he earned fifty cents the first time he played on a streetcorner.

When Alan Lomax from the Library of Congress came to Clarksdale looking for folk singers in 1941, the local people told him that he absolutely had to hear Muddy Waters. Lomax tracked down Muddy and recorded him on a portable machine. When Lomax sent the 78-rpm disc back to Muddy in 1943, Muddy became convinced that he was as good as anyone else out there on the jukebox, and better than most. He decided to hop on board the Illinois Central Railroad and go to Chicago to make a living out of music.

Muddy got his first electric guitar from an uncle in 1944, and adapted quickly to the feel of an instrument that would let him be heard in the noisy Chicago clubs. His talent was immediately recognized on the Chicago blues scene. Soon he had joined the prestigious Sonny Boy Williamson band, and was introduced to Leonard Chess of Chess Records. Chess was impressed with Muddy's talent, but was completely surprised when "I Can't Be Satisfied" was a runaway hit in 1948!

From then on, Muddy got his own band together and played the best clubs in Chicago and across the country. In 1953, he recorded "Hoochie Coochie Man," which sold over 4,000 copies in the first week, and spent several weeks on the Rhythm and Blues Top Ten Chart. He toured extensively around the world, and won Grammy Awards for Best Ethnic/Traditional recording in 1971, 1972, and 1975. His singular delivery of the blues from country fields to city streets created a bridge in American music that supported rock pioneers in their quest for an authentic sound.

Muddy Waters died in Chicago on April 30, 1983, at the age of 68. His music is still inspiring musicians around the world today. It is simply impossible to trace the roots of American music without coming across the name of the man who took blues into the soul of so many across the globe—Muddy Waters.

Books to checkout!

Can't Be Satisfied: The Life and Times of Muddy Waters by Robert Gordon
Muddy Waters: The Mojo Man by Sandra Tooze

Ida B. Wells-Barnett
Anti-Lynching Crusader, Feminist, Publisher

We refuse to believe this country, so powerful to defend its citizens abroad, is unable to protect its citizens at home.

Ida B. Wells was the original pistol packin' mama of civil rights, a crusader for equality with indomitable spirit that led a campaign against the rapaciousness and brutality of lynch mobs. Born into slavery in 1862, to James and Elizabeth Wells, she was a native of Holly Springs, Mississippi. There, she attended Shaw University, the school her father helped to start immediately after the Civil War, which was later known as Rust College.

Tragedy struck Ida at sixteen, when yellow fever consumed both her parents, leaving her to raise her five younger siblings. She did so by teaching at a nearby school, adopting a grueling schedule for more than two years. When she turned eighteen, her widowed Aunt Fannie invited her to stay at her place in Memphis, where she taught school in the adjacent town of Woodstock. By 1884, she had qualified to teach in the Memphis public schools and Aunt Fannie had moved to Washington, D.C., leaving Ida alone in Memphis to teach children while studying at Fisk University and LeMoyne Institute. A year earlier, the Supreme

Court had ruled that the 1875 Civil Rights Act was unlawful, and southern segregation was becoming more and more oppressive. Ida learned about the implications of this ruling when she went to board a first-class Chesapeake & Ohio Railroad car and the conductor asked her to sit in the inferior black car. When he put his hand on her, she bit him hard enough to draw blood, but was unable to avoid being thrown off the train. Ida decided to file suit, and successfully sued the C&O Railroad, winning $500 in damages. Her letters to the editor of a black church periodical, *The Living Way*, drew a lot of attention to her cause and her articulate, forceful writing style. Her articles, written under the pen name Iola, were soon published weekly. By 1886, she was syndicated in black papers across the country; the *Age*, Detroit's *Plaindealer*, Indianapolis' *Freeman*, the Little Rock *Sun*, and others. She became known as the "Princess of the Press," and by 1889, she had bought an interest in the Memphis *Free Speech and Headlight*.

Because she could be just as critical of blacks' hypocrisy as she was of whites', she raised controversy when she addressed the lack of moral and mental capacity of some of the local teachers in the black schools. She was promptly fired from her position. To make ends meet, she started a speaking tour and subscription drive to make the *Free Speech* a paying proposition. Within a year, she had more than doubled the paper's circulation and was earning as much as her teacher's salary. Through constant travel, Wells was able to see much more of the country, and realize the extent of rampant segregation and brutality throughout the South. The issue really hit home when a close friend,

Thomas Moss, was lynched for defending his Memphis grocery store from white attackers. As blacks swarmed away from Memphis—6,000 left in two months—Wells returned to investigate the history of southern lynching. She decried the practice openly in the *Free Speech*, calling into question whites' popular charge of black male lasciviousness and brutishness as an excuse for lynching. She expressed herself freely in a May, 1892 column when she wrote:

> Nobody in this section believes the old threadbare lie that Negro men rape white women. If Southern white men are not careful, they will over-reach themselves and public sentiment will have a reaction. A conclusion will then be reached which will be very damaging to the moral reputation of their women.

Fortunately, Wells was headed out of town for a speaking tour when the article was published, for when she got to New York, she was told that a white mob had destroyed her newspaper office and press, and lookouts were posted on all the trains looking out for her return. It would be too dangerous for her to return to Memphis.

Not to be deterred, Wells continued her columns about inequality in the *Age* and toured England, spreading the word about American lynching. During her stay there, she crossed paths and intellectual swords with Frances Willard of America's Women's Christian Temperance Union. In order to build support for the burgeoning women's suffrage movement, Willard had attempted to alienate the British from the plight of African Americans with statements like "the grog shop is the center of its power." Wells was able to effectively rebut her slanderous remarks through a heated exchange of letters to the British press.

After her trip overseas, she settled in Chicago to write for the *Chicago Conservator,* which she eventually purchased. She also married the paper's editor, Ferdinand Lee Barnett. In 1895, she published the *Red Record*, a scathing document which recorded race lynching in America and supported the conclusion that lynching was used to terrorize blacks into accepting oppression. In 1896, Ida was present at the first convention of the National Association of Colored Women, a historic meeting which formally launched the black women's club movement.

In 1909, she became one of the founders of the National Association for the Advancement of Colored People, a critical organization for addressing civil rights. In 1929, she made an unsuccessful bid for Illinois State Senate.

Active until the end, her death occurred on March 25, 1931, four months before her 69th birthday. For forty years she had been in the forefront of fighting injustice and barbarism.

Books to check out!

Crusade for Justice: The Autobiography of Ida B. Wells
Ida B. Wells-Barrett and American Reform, 1880–1930 by Patricia Schechter
The Selected Works of Ida B. Wells-Barrett edited by Trudier Harris-Lopez

Oprah Winfrey
Actress, Entrepreneur, Talk-Show Host Extraordinaire

My philosophy is that not only are you responsible for your life,
but doing the best at this moment puts you in the best place for
the next moment.

On January 29, 1954, Kosciusko, Mississippi became the hometown to the most popular talk show host in the twentieth century—Oprah Winfrey. Raised on a farm by her grandmother until she was six, Oprah had a strong sense that her life would be different from her grandmother's, who toiled endlessly to keep the tiny family afloat. It was in her grandmother's care that she first tested her oratorical skills as she rehearsed the sermons of James Weldon Johnson for recital in local churches. By her teens, she was touring the churches of Mississippi, reciting Johnson's sermons.

In 1960, Oprah was sent to Milwaukee, Wisconsin, to be raised by her mother. During her time there, a cousin raped Oprah when she was nine, and she suffered more molestation by a friend of the family and an uncle. Oprah came back to these excruciating personal events later in her life in order to bring the problem of sexual abuse to national attention.

In the meantime, she ran away from home at the age of thirteen, and was sent to a juvenile detention home. Because the home was filled to capacity, authorities sent her to live with her father in Nashville, Tennessee. Her father, Vernon Winfrey, was quite a disciplinarian, and forced her to meet a midnight curfew as well as turn in a completed book report each week. He would not accept merely passing grades from her, but required As on her report card.

While she was living under her father's strict regimen, she also grew up to be quite a looker. In 1971, at the age of sixteen, she was the first black Miss Fire Prevention in Nashville and she won the Miss Black Tennessee pageant. When asked by contest judges what she would do with a million dollars, she blurted out, "I'd be a spending fool!" Fortunately, that was not to be the case.

Oprah's broadcasting career began that same year, when she earned a scholarship to major in Speech Communications and Performing Arts at Tennessee State University. She also picked up a radio mic for the first time at Nashville's WVOL. Two years later, she was offered a position as coanchor on the television news program of the CBS affiliate, WVTF. In 1977, Oprah moved to WJZ, the ABC affiliate in Baltimore. She gained a reputation for ad-libbing on the air at WJZ, and station executives decided to place her on a show that would benefit more from her loquacious nature, a talk show entitled *People Are Talking*. In a few years, her talk show was getting better ratings than the former all-time favorite, *Donahue*.

In 1983, she decided to venture to Chicago, where she hosted *A.M. Chicago*, a morning talk show on Chicago station WLZ-TV. Once again, the show became so successful that it outdrew *Donahue* in the Chicago market. The show became so successful that by 1985, it was renamed the *Oprah Winfrey Show*. During that same year, her memorable role in Steven Spielberg's film production of Alice Walker's *The Color Purple* received Oscar and Golden Globe nominations for dramatic film debut. In 1986, King World productions offered to distribute Oprah's show across the country, and within three weeks of her first nationwide broadcast, the Oprah Winfrey Show was the most popular talk show in the country. Within one year of syndication, her deal with King World made her the richest entertainer in the country as she reaped an estimated $31 million in 1987. That same year, she won a Daytime Emmy for Outstanding Talk/Service Show Host. She won the same award in 1989, and every year from 1991 to 1996. In 1997, her show won the Emmy for Outstanding Talk Show, and in 1998 she won an Emmy for Lifetime Achievement. She has also won a Peabody Award, several NAACP Image Awards, and People's Choice Awards.

Oprah founded Harpo Productions in 1986, and has used the venture to produce her show as well as award winning film adaptations of Gloria Naylor's *Women of Brewster Place* and Toni Morrison's *Beloved*. In 2003, after having created the production company and changing the face of the American talk show, Oprah became the first black woman on *Forbes* magazine's list of billionaires.

Oprah is important not only because of her status as a black billionaire, but for her ability to use the electronic media to capture the public's attention on social issues. Oprah used the bully pulpit of her sky-high ratings to focus the public eye on issues such as child molestation, even uncovering her own history with the issue on nationwide TV.

Oprah also has single-handedly altered the American publishing industry. *Oprah's Book Club* rocketed previously obscure authors into national prominence—inclusion in the Club meant that an author was almost sure to be included on the New York Times' bestseller list. Another venture into the publishing world, *O Magazine* became one of the most successful new magazines in publishing history when she launched it in April 2000.

Oprah is an example of what one can achieve when they use charm, wit, and fortitude to make a way for themselves out of no way. After suffering hardship and abuse, she decided to maintain faith in herself and her abilities.

Books to check out!

Oprah Winfrey Speaks: Insights from the World's Most Influential Voice
Oprah Winfrey: A Voice for the People by Philip Brocks

Malcolm X
Activist, Minister, Organizer

Nobody can give you freedom. Nobody can give you equality or justice or anything. If you're a man, you take it.

A reformed predator who turned himself around through religion and caught America's attention with his irresistible oratory skill and unwavering dedication to truth, Malcolm X was, as Ossie Davis said, "our own black, shining Prince."

Malcolm was a man of multiple identities. Aspiring student, thief, pimp, hustler, ex-con, leader, minister, husband, heretic, organizer, militant, and martyr are all terms that have applied to Malcolm, and at one time or other, each one was entirely accurate. An activist who emphasized human rights, Malcolm was reviled and loathed by the American power structure in much the same way as his counterpart in the civil rights struggle, Martin Luther King Jr.

Malcolm Little was born on May 19, 1925 in Omaha, Nebraska to Earl and Louise Norton Little. His mother was a homemaker, his father a Baptist minister. Both were members of the United Negro Improvement Association and supporters of Marcus Garvey, a black nationalist organization that aroused the hatred of local whites. In 1929, their home in Lansing, Michigan was burned to the ground, and in 1931, Earl's mutilated body was found lying across the town's trolley tracks. Louise, suddenly a widow with eight children and no visible means of support, struggled to keep the family together, but eventually had an emotional breakdown and was committed to a mental institution. Her children were scattered to various foster homes and orphanages.

Malcolm was at the top of his class when he graduated from junior high. He then felt the crushing discouragement that many students of color felt, when a teacher told Malcolm that his dream of becoming a lawyer was "no realistic goal for a nigger." He dropped out of school and spent some time with his aunt in Boston, Massachusetts, getting wise to the ways of the street. Eventually, he ventured to neon-tinted streets of Harlem, New York, where he became a hustler, pimp, thief, and gambler under the nickname "Detroit Red."

The scheming and scamming of his hustler lifestyle led to a seven-year prison sentence in 1946. During his time behind bars, a time when he was called "Devil" for his unrepentant resistance to prison authority, he met representatives of the Nation of Islam, the black nationalist organization led by Elijah Muhammad. By the time he was paroled in 1952, he had undergone another transformation: he had dropped his surname, inherited from a slave owner, and replaced it with X, a common NOI appellation that represents the lost history of African people in the United States.

For a little over a dozen years, Malcolm worked in the Nation of

Islam, building mosques in Detroit and Harlem. He made the most of newspaper columns, radio, and television to deliver the Nation of Islam's message across the United States, and eventually became a minister and national spokesperson for the organization. His compelling and down-to-earth speaking style enabled him to convey complex messages in simple, easy to understand parables that moved audiences and attracted recruits across the United States, building the NOI's membership to over 30,000 by the early 60s. His analogies could make an audience laugh out loud, shake their heads in amazement, and then nod in recognition of the challenges facing them in a struggle for independence.

> You got a bad habit. You're hooked and don't know it. You got what's known as "White's Disease". You think you can't get along without the white man. You think you can't get some clothes without the white man. You think you can't get a house without the white man. You think you can't even get a job without the white man. You're worse than the man who thinks he can't get along without heroin. You're worse than the man who thinks he can't get along without morphine. *You're worse than the junkie*, you're in worse shape than the junkie because, the junkie only has a little monkey on his back and your running around with a big white ape named Uncle Sam on your back.

In 1958, Malcolm married Betty Shabazz, and they had three daughters together. In 1959, Mike Wallace created an expose on the NOI, *The Hate That Hate Produced*. The documentary explored the organization's philosophy, and Malcolm featured heavily in the show as the organization's spokesperson. The show catapulted Malcolm and NOI into the living rooms of America, resulting in much more scrutiny from major media. The FBI and CIA also stepped up their assiduous surveillance of Malcolm, Elijah Muhammad, and other members of the NOI in order to spread discontent in the organization.

When President John F. Kennedy was assassinated in 1963, Malcolm compared it to a case of "chickens come home to roost." The analogy was not well received by the general population, nor was it by Elijah Muhammad, who silenced Malcolm for ninety days, forbidding him to assume his duties as spokesperson and minister. By this time, Malcolm had learned of Elijah's relationships with several young women in the NOI—affairs that had resulted in progeny that the leader did not financially support. He was disillusioned with Muhammad and the NOI, and formally left the organization in 1964. That same year, he took a pilgrimage to Mecca and transformed once again, changing his name to El Hajj Malik El Shabazz, and adopting the mainstream Sunni Islam as his religious creed. He wrote of his transformation in his Letter from Mecca:

> America needs to understand Islam, because this is the one religion that erases from its society the race problem. Throughout my travels in the Muslim world, I have met, talked to, and even eaten with people who in America would have been considered white—but the white attitude was removed from their minds by the religion of Islam. I have never before seen sincere and true brotherhood practiced by all colors together, irrespective of their color.

He founded a new organization, **Muslim Mosque, Inc.,** designed to continue the work of organizing black people across the world for social and political change.

When Malcolm returned, he was denounced as a traitor to the NOI, and received death threats on a regular basis. His home in East Elmhurst, New York, like the one of his youth in Michigan, was set afire in the middle of the night, and bodyguards surrounded him wherever he went. Malcolm remained undeterred. On February 21, 1965, three gunmen from the NOI rushed Malcolm onstage at Manhattan's Audubon Ballroom and shot him fifteen times at close range.

Fortunately, just before his assassination, he had been working closely with Alex Haley to document his life. The result, *Autobiography of Malcolm X,* is essential to understanding the black human rights struggle in America.

While Malcolm is popular today, with his face on government stamps, and his X emblazoned onto caps and T-shirts in the mid-90s, it is important to remember that while he was alive, he was scorned and rebuked by naysayers from most sectors of the American public, black and white. Nevertheless, he never stopped searching for truth, and was unafraid of changing his perspective, to say, "I was wrong," in order to pursue that truth. When we study Malcolm's legacy, we study our true capacity for change through an unrelenting search for truth, regardless of the circumstances.

Books to check out!

Malcolm X Speaks: Selected Speeches and Statements ed. by George Breitman
Malcolm X: The Last Speeches ed. by Bruce Perry
Malcolm X Talks to Young People
The Judas Factor by Karl Evanzz

Black on Black Love

A fact: when we read the newspapers, watch TV and movies, or listen to the radio, we almost never hear stories about black-on-black love. Usually what we hear are stories of murder, crime, rape, and treachery; broadcast to anyone around the world that will listen. This can make it hard to believe that black folks can still ever rely on each other for anything: honesty, integrity, respect, friendship, or that most important ingredient, love. Romantic love, familial love, brotherly love, sisterly love, and love of any gender combination in the black community seem to be under massive assault in America.

Because the rest of this book is about answers and facts, it seems fitting to end with a section that is all about questions—the question of black-on-black love. What is it? Does it exist? Is it endangered? Will it survive? Does it still beat back slavery, the way that it did when Harriet led her passengers on the northward bound freedom train? Does it still withstand the test of sons, daughters, grandmas, aunts, and uncles being sold off to oblivion in the blink of an eye? Does it hold up to the test of self-sacrifice by men like King and women like Wells? When it stumbles, will it rise up again the way Fannie Lou Hamer got up from a Winona, Mississippi jail cell floor? Will it keep on marching the way she did, step after step toward opportunity at a voting booth? Does black-on-black love still write and agitate with the fervor and purpose of W.E.B. Du Bois, or stand on the steps of its own memorial and sing like Marian Anderson? Will this love redefine itself; reshape itself as it learns more about the world, the way Malcolm changed from Little to Red to X to Shabazz? The way Cassius became Muhammad? The way Audre became Zami became Gamba Adisa? The way Negro became Black became African American? What does black love look like in the 21st century? How will we raise our black-on-black love? How will we celebrate black-on-black love beyond Kwanzaa, beyond Black History Month? Will we feed our bodies and our minds the best food available? Do we black-on-black love enough to start and support our own institutions?

These are questions that can only be answered by black folks in the course of our everyday actions: in the way we chill with each other, the way we respect each other, the way we lift each other up and the way we help each other out. While this book does highlight some individuals, black survival, progress, and triumph have always been due to black folks working together toward common goals. Martin would not be Martin if it were not for those who helped him organize. Tubman would have gotten nowhere without the help of those who helped run the Underground Railroad. Isn't that a special kind of love that we should maintain in the future? How will we make that love survive? The answer, dear reader, is in the hearts and hands of black folks.

About the Author

Tyehimba Jess, a Detroit native, is a poet, fiction writer, teacher, blues lover, and researcher currently living in Brooklyn. Jess's writing has appeared in *Dark Matter 2, Beyond The Frontier: African American Poetry for the Twenty-First Century, Role Call: A Generational Anthology of Social and Political Black Literature and Art, Bum Rush the Page: A Def Poetry Jam, Power Lines: Ten Years of Poetry from Chicago's Guild Complex, Slam: The Art of Performance Poetry, Ploughshares, Mosaic Magazine, Obsidian III: Literature in the African Diaspora, Warpland: A Journal of Black Literature and Ideas,* and various other publications.